TECHNICAL COLLEGE OF THE LOWCOUNTRY
LEARNING RESOURCES CENTER
POST OFFICE BOX 1288
BEAUFORT, SOUTH CAROLINA 29901-1288

Twayne's United States Authors Series

Sylvia E. Bowman, *Editor*

INDIANA UNIVERSITY

Ring Lardner

RING LARDNER

by WALTON R. PATRICK

Auburn University

 32

Twayne Publishers, Inc.   ::   New York

MANUFACTURED IN THE UNITED STATES OF AMERICA BY
UNITED PRINTING SERVICES, INC.
NEW HAVEN, CONN.

For
EARL L. BRADSHER
EMERITUS PROFESSOR OF AMERICAN LITERATURE
LOUISIANA STATE UNIVERSITY

Preface

RING LARDNER occupies a singularly interesting position in American literature. He provides the unusual example of a writer who not only entered the serious literary world through the pages of mass-circulation periodicals but who also remained closely associated with popular journalism throughout his career. Had he continued writing fiction about comic baseball players, this association would hardly be remarkable, for the sports page—and Lardner himself had long been connected with it—had created a large and appreciative audience for stories dealing with sports and athletes. But as he progressed in his career, he directed his attention to other equally distinctive phases of American life and to other common American character types, virtually discontinuing his stories about sports and athletes. Moreover, as he enlarged the scope of his fiction, he increasingly displayed in it a severely critical tone.

As the result of this development, Lardner won recognition in the 1920's as one of the most biting satirists of American life the country had produced. At the same time, however, he retained his earlier reputation as a humorist and popular journalist. This circumstance may explain why the editors of such magazines as the *Saturday Evening Post, Redbook, Hearst's International Cosmopolitan,* and *Liberty* avidly sought his works and published even his harshest, most critical stories in their pages. The large public following he attracted through the magazines evidently missed the deeper import of his fiction and read it as humor—not a surprising fact, perhaps, for in these magazines and similar ones he regularly published humorous articles and sketches. But the more discerning audience which he reached primarily through the book collections of his fiction attached a different meaning to his stories and regarded him as a ferocious, coldly impersonal satirist. This latter group included such influential critics of the day as H. L. Mencken, Carl Van Doren, Edmund Wilson, Stuart Sherman, and Gilbert Seldes.

If many of the first group of readers mistakenly read his

fiction as humor only, some of the serious literary critics in the second group were equally mistaken in regarding it as the work of a misanthrope. Though Lardner produced much excellent humorous writing, he was no mere humorist; but, despite having written some of the most sardonic short stories to be found in the entire range of American literature, neither was he a hater of mankind. Rather, he was an acutely sensitive idealist disturbed by the deviations of the real world in which he lived from a better or more ideal world that might be possible if human beings were less prone than they are to self-delusion, pretentiousness, and hypocrisy. Cloaking his inner attitudes with silence, he simply reported life as he saw it, repeatedly insisting that he just "listened hard."

If Lardner produced a great quantity of ephemeral writing, this fact is surely much less significant than his more than 120 short stories, the best of which place him in the front rank of the masters of the American short story. In addition, he placed the stamp of a distinguished literary talent on a substantial quantity of his nonfiction.

This study has the aim of describing and evaluating Lardner's literary achievement. The introductory chapter traces his development as a writer and relates the distinctly native American quality of his work to the circumstances of his life, the purpose being to show that the American milieu he experienced strongly influenced the matter and method of his writing as well as his outlook. Chapters II and III discuss the groups of related stories he wrote centering on Jack Keefe, the rookie baseball pitcher; on Fred Gross, a Chicago police detective; and on "Gullible" and Tom Finch, two "wise boobs." Chapters IV and V discuss the separate short stories collected in *How to Write Short Stories, The Love Nest and Other Stories,* and *Round Up;* and Chapter VI briefly considers thirty-nine of Lardner's uncollected stories. Chapter VII treats some of Lardner's most important nonfiction, and the final chapter surveys his reputation and literary position. Though Lardner's nonfiction merits more attention than is here given to it, it seemed advisable, within the space available, to place the primary emphasis on the fiction.

Acknowledgments

In preparing this work, I have incurred obligations to many persons: To Donald Elder who responded to questions and who provided through his *Ring Lardner, A Biography* the single most valuable aid to this study; to Howard Webb, Jr., who supplied me with a copy of his Lardner bibliography; to my colleagues Eugene Current-Garcia, Carl Benson, and Peter D. Zivkovic, who offered valuable suggestions on my manuscript; to Carolyn Bates, who typed it; and to the Auburn University library staff for assisting me in securing the library materials needed. Finally, the Auburn University Research Grant-in-Aid program supplied funds for travel to libraries and for purchase of microfilm and photostatic copies of some of Lardner's works.

To Charles Scribner's Sons I express appreciation for permission to quote from Lardner's *You Know Me Al, The Big Town, How to Write Short Stories, The Love Nest and Other Stories, What of It?*, and *First and Last;* to *Redbook* magazine for permission to quote from uncollected Lardner stories; To Donald Elder and Doubleday and Company for permission to quote from *Ring Lardner, A Biography;* to Mrs. Ludwig Lewisohn, literary executrix for Ludwig Lewisohn's Estate, for permission to quote from *Expression in America;* to Mrs. Sherwood Anderson and Harold Ober Associates for permission to quote from Sherwood Anderson's *No Swank* and *Notebook;* to The Viking Press for permission to quote from Gilbert Seldes's introduction to *The Portable Ring Lardner;* and to Mr. Leonard Woolf for permission to quote from Virginia Woolf's *The Moment and Other Essays.* I make grateful acknowledgment also to *The American Quarterly,* Duke University Press, Alfred A. Knopf, Inc., Houghton Mifflin Company, *The New Republic, The Reporter, The Saturday Review,* and Scott, Foresman and Company for permission to quote from copyrighted material, as cited in detail in the footnotes. Brief passages from essays and stories published in *The Saturday Evening Post* (© by The Curtis Publishing Company) are reprinted by special permision of that publication.

Contents

Chronology

1885 Ringgold Wilmer Lardner born March 6, in Niles, Michigan, the ninth and youngest child of wealthy parents, Henry and Lena Phillips Lardner.

1890- Taught in the home with brother and sister nearest him
1897 in age (Rex and Anna), first by mother and then by tutor. His interest in baseball, music, and theatricals began in this period.

1897- Attended the Niles, Michigan, high school, played foot-
1901 ball, sang in a quartet, wrote class poem, graduated at age sixteen.

1901 Worked briefly in Chicago as office boy, first for the McCormick Harvester Company, later for a real estate firm. Dismissed successively from these jobs, he returned to Niles; worked briefly as "freight hustler" for the Michigan Central Railroad.

1902 In January at father's behest, enrolled with brother Rex, in Armour Institute, Chicago, to study engineering. Both indifferent students; "flunked" out at the end of the spring semester.

1903- Returned to Niles and "rested" a year, working thereafter
1905 about a year and a half as bookkeeper, bill collector, and meter-reader for the Niles Gas Company. Participated in the activities of the Niles American minstrel group, writing the music and most of the lyrics for, as well as acting in, a two-act musical comedy, *Zanzibar*.

1905- Reporter for the South Bend, Indiana, *Times*, fall of 1905
1907 to November, 1907.

1907- November to February, general sports writer for the
1908 Chicago *Inter-Ocean*. February to November, baseball reporter for the Chicago *Examiner*, writing under the paper's alias of "James Clarkson." Assigned in March to travel with the Chicago White Sox on their spring tour and to cover their games for the season.

1908- Baseball reporter for the Chicago *Tribune*, an important
1910   period in the development of his knowledge of ballplayers
and of his abilities as a reporter.

1910- After resigning from the *Tribune* staff in December, 1910,
1911   worked successively as managing editor and feature writer
of the St. Louis *Sporting News;* as sports editor of the
Boston *American;* and as copyreader for the Chicago
American. Married Ellis Abbott, June 28, 1911.

1912   In February, again employed as baseball writer for the
Chicago *Examiner.* His first son, John Abbott, born May 4.

1913   Rejoined the staff of the Chicago *Tribune* on June 3 to
write a daily variety column, "In the Wake of the
News," which he continued for six years.

1914   Published ten stories in *The Saturday Evening Post,* six of
which form the first sequence of stories about Jack Keefe,
the illiterate bush leaguer (collected as *You Know Me Al,*
1916). Collaborated with Edward C. Heeman in publishing
a souvenir booklet, *March 6th: The Home Coming of
Charles A. Comiskey, John J. McGraw and James J.
Callahan,* commemorating the return of the Chicago White
Sox and New York Giants from a world tour. His second
son, James Phillips, born May 18. Bought home in Riverside, a west suburb of Chicago. His father dies.

1915   Published a second sequence of Jack Keefe stories in
The Saturday Evening Post; initiated a new sequence in
the *Redbook* dealing with Fred Gross, a Chicago police
detective; and published other stories and articles in
the *American, McClure's,* and *Metropolitan* as well as
Bib Ballads, a thin volume of humorous verse about
children. His third son, Ringgold Wilmer, Jr., born
August 19.

1916- Published more Fred Gross stories and introduced yet
1917   another character type in a sequence of stories which
appeared in 1917 as *Gullible's Travels, Etc.* Sold his
Chicago Riverside home in the spring of 1917 and made a
brief trip to France as war correspondent for *Collier's*
in August of 1917.

1918   Wrote nine additional Jack Keefe stories, taking Jack into the army and overseas, most of them collected in *Treat 'Em Rough* (1918) and *The Real Dope* (1919).

1919   Published *Own Your Own Home,* a collection of four of the Fred Gross stories; *Regular Fellows I Have Met,* a book of comic verse about prominent business and professional men; and the final sequence of Jack Keefe stories. Resigned in June from the *Tribune* staff, and began writing a weekly column for John N. Wheeler's Bell Syndicate in the autumn, when family moved to Greenwich, Connecticut. Fourth son, David, born, March 11.

1920-
1921   Published a sequence of five stories in *The Saturday Evening Post,* which soon reappeared as *The Big Town* (1921). In early spring, moved to Great Neck, Long Island. Published *Young Immigrunts* (1920) and *Symptoms Of Being 35* (1921).

1922-
1924   Wrote little fiction but began contributing sketches to the Follies, though without notable success. Wrote text for a comic strip based on Jack Keefe from October, 1923, to the following fall. Under Fitzgerald's prompting, published *How to Write Short Stories* [*With Samples*] in 1924.

1925   Published *What of It?,* a collection of humorous pieces which had first appeared in periodicals. Scribner's reissued *You Know Me Al, Gullible's Travels,* and *The Big Town.*

1926-
1927   Published *The Love Nest and Other Stories* (1926), his second major collection, and *The Story of a Wonder Man* (1927), a burlesque autobiography. In summer of 1926, discovered he had tuberculosis, a recurrent malady thereafter. Stopped writing the Bell Syndicate column in March, 1927, to devote more time to theatrical writing.

1928-
1930   Moved to East Hampton, Long Island, where he and Grantland Rice had built houses on adjacent lots. Collaborated with George M. Cohan on *Elmer, the Great,* a play which failed. Alarmed at declining income, Lardner again turned to journalism, writing for two months four columns weekly for the new *Telegraph* at the reputed rate of $50,000 per year. Published *Round Up* (1929), a collection

of thirty-five stories. In 1929, collaborated with George S. Kaufman on *June Moon*, his only successful play.

1930-   Despite failing health, requiring frequent hospitalization
1933   and two trips to the West, Lardner produced much work in his last years: In 1930, again writing briefly for the Bell Syndicate; in 1931, a series of autobiographical articles for the *Saturday Evening Post*; in 1932 (for the same periodical), a new Busher series, published as *Lose with a Smile* (1933); and from June, 1932, to August, 1933, a series of radio columns for *The New Yorker*, embodying a mild crusade against pornographic songs and risqué comedians. Died September 25, 1933, of a heart attack.

1934   *First and Last,* edited by Gilbert Seldes.

Ring Lardner

CHAPTER 1

The Matrix of Ring Lardner's Mind and Art

A CLOSE RELATIONSHIP exists between the literary works of Ring Lardner and the circumstances of his life. He lived successively in the small town and the large, the city, and the fashionable suburbs. He became intimately acquainted with three broad, complex, and intensely competitive areas of American life—journalism, professional sports, and the theater, particularly Broadway show business. These backgrounds, populated with illiterate ballplayers, vanity-ridden song writers, morons, wise boobs, and fiends of the bridge table and golf course, supplied him with the entire gallery of characters depicted in his fiction. They also provided him with that accurate knowledge of the American vernacular which is the distinguishing feature of his style, and they influenced the development of the severely realistic and frequently sardonic outlook evident in his work. Moving through a disturbing but distinctively American world of jangled human relationships, Lardner reported what he saw and heard with detachment and objectivity. For this reason, to follow the unfolding stages of his career, even as briefly as they will be narrated in this chapter, is to witness the American environment playing on a sensitive, idealistic temperament to create one of the most thoroughly American writers the country has produced.

I *Youth in Niles: The Formative Years*

Lardner's life story, that of a small-town boy who, with benefit of little formal schooling, came to a serious literary career by the way of newspaper reporting, follows a pattern made familiar by other American writers. It departs from the typical pattern, however, in at least one major particular. Writers such as Mark Twain, Theodore Dreiser, and Sherwood Anderson enjoyed little family security in their youths and were compelled to face the hard realities of life from early ages. By contrast, Lardner was the son of wealthy, well-educated parents; and during the first twenty years of his life, from his birth in 1885 to the time he became a newspaper reporter in 1905, he led a sheltered, idealistic existence, enjoying the advantages of a luxurious, indulgent, and cultivated family environment.

Lardner was born March 6, 1885, in Niles, Michigan, the last of the nine children of Henry and Lena Phillips Lardner. Henry Lardner, a member of the second generation of the Lardner family to live in the Niles area, traced his ancestry to Lynford Lardner who had migrated from England and settled in Philadelphia in 1740. Lena Phillips, Ring's mother, was the witty, charming daughter of an Episcopal rector, the Reverend Joseph Phillips, whom Donald Elder described in his biography of Lardner as "a fine scholar and a man of far greater intellect than was common among clergymen in small midwestern parishes."[1] The basis of the family fortune was land which Henry Lardner had inherited from his father and his sister, a fortune he expanded through his own efforts until a business failure in 1901 wiped it out.

In company with Rex and Anna, the brother and the sister nearest him in age, Ring spent his childhood in the family home on Bond Street, a large, comfortable dwelling located on spacious grounds and enclosed with a rail fence. The family circle, under the animated guidance of his talented mother—she wrote plays, poems, and stories—was lively, harmonious, and happy. The children had nursemaids when they were young, and a coachman to take them driving. They invented and acted in childish theatricals, one of which was a dramatic recitation of Poe's "The Raven" in which "the owl-eyed Ring, perched on a bookcase, quoth 'nevermore' at appropriate intervals" (Elder, 16). Music was a favorite family pastime, the music room of the Lardner home being equipped with a pipe organ and two pianos; and from an early age, Ring displayed an aptitude for music. Baseball, however, figured prominently among his childhood interests. He later wrote that he and Rex "could rattle off the batting order of any of the National League's twelve clubs" even when he and Rex were still being pushed around Niles in their perambulators,[2] a statement probably not greatly exaggerated. Three of his lifelong interests—theatricals, music, and baseball—were thus formed in his childhood.

Ring, together with Rex and Anna, received his early schooling in the home because ". . . us 3 youngest members of the family was too fragile to mingle with the tough eggs from the West Side and the Dickerell."[3] At first their mother taught them, but as they grew older a tutor was employed to instruct them in Latin, mathematics, and geography. The atmosphere that prevailed during these lessons is suggested by Lardner's later statement: "We had a private tutor that come to the house every morning at 9 and stayed till noon and on acct. of it taking him 2 and a ½ hrs. to get us to stop giggling, why they was only a ½ hr. left for work and this was generally always spent on penmanship which was his passion." It is not surprising that all three children failed the entrance examinations to the local high school, though they were admitted anyway. In high school, where "most of we boys done our studying at a 10 x 5 table with side pockets in it," Lardner, however, did well in his studies, sang in a local quartet, played football during his junior and senior years, and wrote the senior class poem. When he graduated in 1901 at the age of sixteen, he "had mastered just enough of one live foreign language to tell Razzle, a gullible bartender, that [he] war ein and Zwanzig jahre alt."

Having no specific career in mind and apparently as much intent on fun as anything else, Lardner spent the next four years in a rather aimless manner—a transition period in which he grew to maturity and gradually prepared to move from the closely knit family circle to the outside world. Following graduation from high school, he worked briefly in Chicago as an office boy, first for the McCormick Harvester Company and then for a real estate firm. "Canned" in succession from both of these jobs, he returned to Niles to work as a freight hustler for a railroad, "where I learned that they's only one thing worse to unload than a carload of iron pipe and that is a carload of hides."[4] But he was also soon dismissed from this job "for putting a box of cheese in the through Jackson car, when common sense should have told me that it ought to go to Battle Creek."[5]

In January, 1902, Lardner's father made an effort to push him toward a career by sending him, with Rex, to the Armour Institute in Chicago to study mechanical engineering, a subject in which neither he nor Rex had the least interest. The two boys did their "studying" at the theaters and in bars, and both flunked out at the end of the semester, though Ring passed in rhetoric. Back in Niles, while "resting" from "the strain which had wrought havoc with my nervous system,"[6] Lardner joined the local minstrel group, and during the next year and a half, participated in at least two shows.[7] The most successful of these was *Zanzibar,* a two-act musical comedy, for which Lardner wrote the music and most of the lyrics in addition to appearing himself in the show as an actor and singer (Elder, 30-31). In 1904, he began working for the Niles Gas Company at $5.00 per week, his duties being "to read meters, make out bills, keep books, try to collect bad debts . . . handle all moneys, get new customers and mop the office floor at least once daily."[8] He held this job for nearly two years, and it must have served as a finishing school for his knowledge of the small town besides introducing him to less pleasant phases of human conduct. For he later wrote: " I learned one thing on this job—that there's a lot of cheating done in the gas business, and it's all done by the consumer. The gas company doesn't have to cheat."[9] He added further that when he was first hired as a reporter he "had no newspaper experience, but a two years' course in a gas-office teaches you practically all there is to know about human nature."[10]

The period of Lardner's permanent residence in Niles came to an end in the fall of 1905, when he became a reporter for the South Bend, Indiana, *Times.* Now twenty years of age, he was a tall, shy person who had already formed the solemn, mask-like demeanor behind which he concealed his real feelings throughout his adult life.[11] As the indulged, protected child of wealthy parents he had grown up viewing life from the vantage point of a person with a superior position in his community. Though it is hardly possible to agree with the critics who say that Lardner continued to view life from an assumed position of superiority—as one of the elite, a snob—it is nevertheless evident that the harmonious, affectionate home environment he became conditioned to in his youth provided him with a standard for measuring human conduct. The discordant family relationships and the pettiness and meanness of domestic life pictured in his fiction are the direct opposites of what Lardner experienced in his early life. He may have found the real world of his adulthood worse than it actually was because he measured it in part by the ideal world of his youth.

II *From Cub Reporter to Columnist*

The first major stage of Lardner's professional career began in 1905, when he became a cub reporter, and extended to 1913, when he became a newspaper columnist for the Chicago *Tribune*. In his progression from cub reporting to big-city journalism, he acquired the thorough knowledge of professional baseball players on which the stories bringing him his early fame were based; he thoroughly mastered the American vernacular which became his trademark as a fiction writer; and he developed the technique of writing "in character"—that is, as a ballplayer, wise boob, or whatnot. Viewed in the perspective of his journalistic career, the busher stories he began publishing in 1914 were not a new turn in his development as a writer but rather the logical—one might almost say, the inevitable—culmination of his development.

It was entirely by accident that Lardner became a reporter. An editor of the South Bend *Times*, Edgar Stoll, came to Niles intending to offer a job to Rex, then a writer for the Niles newspaper and a correspondent for the South Bend *Tribune*, a competitor of the *Times*. Finding Rex on vacation, Stoll sought information about him from Ring. When Ring learned the reporting job paid $12.00 a week, or $4.00 a week more than he was then earning with the gas company, and knowing that Rex was under contract, he suggested himself for the job and was employed.[12] His initial assignments on the paper included being "society reporter, court-house man, dramatic critic and sporting editor."[13]

As a beginning journalist Lardner, according to Stoll, was far from brilliant. "Of all the fellows I've tried to break into reporting . . .," he said in 1933, "Ring Lardner was the world's worst. It just seemed that he couldn't catch on." Stoll would have fired him, he said, except that "everybody liked him so well personally I couldn't bring myself to it."[14] However, Donald Elder, Lardner's biographer, scoffs at this statement. "As a matter of fact," Elder says, "he became a very good reporter in South Bend, and the *Times* never had a better baseball writer. For $12.00 a week it had a genius." In support of his position, Elder quotes in his biography one of Lardner's earliest baseball stories, pointing out that it displayed the characteristics of his later sports stories: the centering of the story on "a personality or a single dramatic play" instead of giving the stringy inning-by-inning account typical of the usual sports story (Elder, 38-41). In any case, after two years on the *Times,* Lardner had learned both reporting and professional baseball well enough to want to move up to a larger paper and to the major baseball league.

In the fall of 1907, he secured a job at $18.50 a week as general sports writer for the Chicago *Inter-Ocean;* but he served only a brief apprenticeship in city journalism on that paper before he moved in February, 1908, to the Chicago *Examiner.* As baseball writer for the *Examiner,* he traveled with the Chicago White Sox on their 1908 spring tour and covered their games for the season, the first of many such assignments. Living with the players on pullmans and in hotels, witnessing their characteristic behavior on field and off, and hearing constantly the special idiom they spoke, Lardner began his intensive education in ballplayers, an education continued through the next five years, so that finally he came to know them, inside and out, as well as anyone ever could. One player whom he met on the 1908 trip may have figured prominently in the genesis of his famous busher, Jack Keefe. He was an illiterate infielder who drafted Lardner as his secretary, "a spare-time job I . . . held, off and on, for two or three years."[15] Lardner not only read aloud to the player the menus, the daily sports news, and the letters from his wife "Myrtle," but he also typed out replies to Myrtle at the player's dictation. Lardner recalled that one of these went as follows:

> "Well I guess you better tell her where we are first. No. Start out this way: 'Dear Myrt.' And then tell her she knows damn well I don't get no pay till the last of April, and nothing then because I already drawed ahead. Tell her to borrow off Edith von Driska, and she can pay her back the first of May. Tell her I never felt better in my life and looks like I will have a great year, if they's nothing to worry me like worrying about money. Tell her the weather's been great, just like summer, only them two days it rained in Birmingham. It rained a couple days in Montgomery and a week in New Orleans. My old souper feels great. Detroit is the club we got to beat—them and Cleveland and St. Louis, and maybe the New York club. Oh, you know what to tell her. You know what they like to hear."[16]

Lardner was popular with the players and participated in their poker games, singing, and other hotel and pullman pastimes.

As much as he liked them, he was nevertheless the amused but solemn-faced observer of their idiosyncrasies and antics; he was storing up in his mind, consciously or not, material he would later use in fiction.

In the fall of 1908, when the baseball season was over, Lardner changed jobs again, this time joining the staff of the *Tribune,* Chicago's largest paper. During the next two years, he was periodically assigned to travel with one or another of the Chicago ball clubs. He apparently developed a special liking for the Cubs, "a salty, humorous, quarrelsome, opinionated, and loquacious bunch," who supplied him for two seasons with "hilarious copy and high entertainment" (Elder, 61). He also covered other sports events in the off-season for baseball, particularly football, coming thus to know other types of athletes, both amateur and professional. In this period, as his reporting abilities reached maturity, Lardner began using more humor and irony in his news stories than he had used in his earlier Chicago reporting but he had not yet begun writing in the vernacular, though he had been using it in his personal correspondence for several years.[17]

While still working on the South Bend *Times,* Lardner had met Ellis Abbot of Goshen, Indiana, in 1907, and, though seeing her only occasionally in Goshen or Chicago, he had courted her steadily through correspondence written chiefly in verse and often signed "Ringlets."[18] When they finally became engaged in 1910, he began seeking a job which involved less travel and more salary. In December, 1910, he resigned from the *Tribune* to become managing editor of the St. Louis *Sporting News,* but he soon left it to become sports editor of the *Boston American.* Leaving that position in less than a year, he returned to Chicago to serve for a time as copyreader for the *American* before he again, in 1912, became baseball writer for the *Examiner.* Despite his not yet having secured the kind of position he desired, he and Ellis were married on June 28, 1911, and subsequently became the parents of four boys: John (1912), James (1914), Ringgold Wilmer, Jr. (1915), and David (1918).

III *Columnist and Short Story Writer*

The second major phase of Lardner's career began in 1913 when he rejoined the staff of the *Tribune* to conduct the "In the Wake of the News" column on the sports page. It ended in 1919, when Lardner, now famous as a columnist and story writer, resigned from the *Tribune*, moved from Chicago to New York, and became a columnist for the Bell Syndicate.

The "Wake" column, which Lardner wrote from June 3, 1913, to June 20, 1919, occupies a place of special importance in his development as a writer. For one thing, despite the growing needs of his steadily increasing family, it brought him a reasonably adequate income: his starting salary of $75.00 a week had increased within three years to $200 a week; for another, even though a daily column took its toll of his creative energy, it allowed him time for other writing. Most important, however, it gave him an outlet for experimenting daily in print with the whole variety of techniques and forms he thereafter used in his fiction and other works. Giving free rein to his talent for humor, irony, and satire, he wrote for the column comic playlets, verse, parodies, burlesque novels, and "short stories" (Elder, 95). And almost from the first, he began using vernacular in the column, as Howard W. Webb, Jr., shows in his perceptive article, "The Lardner Idiom."[19] In tracing the development of the idiom through the "Wake" column, Webb notes that Lardner first used it in "The Pennant Pursuit," a "novel," purporting to be written by the copy boy, which began appearing just nine days after Lardner took over the column. Soon after, he ran a piece written "by a athlete" who gives an "unassisted" account of a ball game in his own language—unassisted, that is, by a ghost writer—and "by the end of 1913 the idiom had become a staple part of 'In the Wake of the News.'"

With little effort, Lardner shifted from writing stories for the "Wake" column in which an athlete "unassisted" tells a story in his own idiom, to writing full-length short stories in which a rookie ballplayer narrates his adventures in the big league in letters written in his own language to his hometown friend, Al. After minor difficulty in placing the first story, Lardner published the initial sequence of six in the *Saturday Evening Post* from March 7 to November 7, 1914. In their satiric portrait of a vain, idiotic, illiterate ballplayer, these stories assaulted the popular image of the athlete enshrined in the hearts of devoted fans; yet they were well received by *Post* readers, no doubt because they were merely regarded as humor. The next year Lardner published another group of five in which he imaginatively took his blustering, harebrained hero on the world tour which the White Sox and Giants had recently made to promote baseball as an international game. In two other series, published in 1918 and collected in book form as *Treat 'Em Rough* and *The Real Dope,* he took his character into an army training camp and then overseas as a soldier. In a final group, published in 1919, Jack Keefe doffed his soldier's uniform and resumed his struggles in the big league. Thus, between March 7, 1914, and October 13, 1919, Lardner published a total of twenty-six Jack Keefe stories; and in 1921, before he forever abandoned his perpetual rookie, he wrote the text for a comic-strip representation of him.

Despite their number, the Jack Keefe stories constituted less than half of the fiction Lardner wrote between 1914 and 1919, a highly productive period for him, particularly in view of his daily column and the other nonfiction he produced. Many of his stories of these years, besides those concerned with Jack Keefe, also deal with athletes, most frequently with professional ballplayers, but sometimes with prize fighters or college football players, and in one case, with businessmen golfers. Beginning in 1915, however, he steadily expanded the range of his fiction to other character types and other areas of activity. At the same time, though he was already reaching a national audience through the pages of the *Saturday Evening Post,* he began publishing in other mass-circulation periodicals and increased still further the size of his reading public.

One of his early departures from the sporting world was a group of stories which began appearing in 1915 and which centered on a Chicago police detective, Fred Gross. It is true that neither in the traits of the main character nor in the technique used to present him are the stories very far removed from those about Keefe, for Gross is a dumb boob who narrates his adventures in letters to his brother "Charley." Still, the stories are not about Gross's efforts to make good in his profession but about his stumble-bum attempts to get along harmoniously with his neighbors in the suburban community where he lives—above all, to win the approval of the socially elite members of that community. Thus with the Gross stories (four of which were later collected in *Own Your Own Home*), Lardner moved to another phase of life as typically American as the ball-park, the world of suburbia and suburbanites. If it was a world he then knew less well than he did the sports' world, it was nevertheless one with which he was personally acquainted, for in 1914 he had purchased a home in Riverside, a west suburb of Chicago, where he continued to live until 1917.

In yet another group of stories which began appearing in 1916–the third major sequence Lardner was now working on–he introduced a character quite different from either Keefe or Gross: the wise boob, the main character of *Gullible's Travels.* Gullible tells his stories rather than writes them; and, being more intelligent than Keefe or Gross, he speaks a witty, racy vernacular. Broadly speaking, he is representative of an average American type: the "bright guy," usually in the know or thinking that he is, he holds a good opinion of himself and is quite willing to let others share it, particularly those with more money and a higher social status. Under different names, this character type appears in a number of Lardner's stories and even serves as an "in-character" mask for Lardner in much of his nonfiction.

Besides the Grosses, Gullibles, and all kinds of athletes, Lardner populated his stories of this period with characters as varied as tourists, stenographers, practical jokers, soldiers, bickering couples, young businessmen, and heavy drinkers. Despite the fact that his gallery of characters was yet far from complete and that his technique still lacked the variety it was to exhibit later, Lardner wrote some of his best fiction in these years.

His chief nonfiction of the period, aside from his column, consisted of articles on baseball and its heroes for the *American* and of another group of pieces done on assignment as a war correspondent for *Collier's,* an assignment which took him to France for four weeks. In France, he spent most of his time fighting army red-tape, and came no closer to front-line trenches than a view of them through field glasses, though he was allowed to visit a rear-area training camp. While he converted the experiences of the trip into passably humorous copy, he apparently did so with great effort; he was "miscast in the role of war correspondent" and knew that "he couldn't kid a war" (Elder, 149).

One other work of nonfiction serves as a rather curious postscript to Lardner's writing of this period: *Regular Fellows I Have Met,* a book of verse about prominent business and professional men, mostly of the Chicago area. The verse–a quatrain for each person–accompanies full-page cartoons of the subjects, who are often shown rolling up their sleeves to perform an altruistic civic deed but more frequently appear on the golf course, at the ball game, or in the trout stream. All are highly successful Americans, the pillars of the civic and business life of their city, but they are "regular fellows" sharing the fondness of the rank and file American for sports and the outdoors. In the verses, Lardner pokes good-natured fun at his subjects, the kind typical of civic clubs or business groups, where kidding is a form of flattery or the means of showing approval. Within a few years, Lardner would make successful "regular fellows" of this sort the target of stinging satire and would even satirize his own success in *The Story of a Wonder Man*. While he may have written *Regular Fellows* with tongue in cheek, the difference in his treatment of successful men in this and later works reflects a shift in his viewpoint. For even though the image of America and Americans which emerges from his work of the 'teens is hardly a flattering one, it is nevertheless mild and sympathetic when compared with the one presented in his later work.

IV *The Major Period*

The third and most important stage of Lardner's career covers the decade from 1919, when he became a Bell Syndicate columnist, to 1929, when poor health began to affect seriously the quality and volume of his work. At the beginning of this phase of his development, Lardner already possessed a national reputation as a humorist, columnist, and popular writer but not as a serious literary artist. When "discovered" in the 1920's by such important and vocal critics as H. L. Mencken, Gilbert Seldes, H. S. Canby, Edmund Wilson, Carl Van Doren, and Stuart Sherman, however, he won a second reputation as a major satirist of American life—and this in a decade which specialized in criticism of American life. By 1929, though still retaining his popular reputation and publishing only in mass-circulation periodicals, he was everywhere being hailed as one of the country's leading writers.

Some of the encomiums critics heaped on him in this period were ludicrously extravagant: he was, for example, compared with Chekhov, Swift, Twain, G. B. Shaw, and even Shakespeare, in the sense of appealing to both select and popular audiences.[20] It may be, as Delmore Schwartz has suggested, that critics of the period avoided middle-ground positions and saw writers as all good or all bad.[21] Or it may be that the literary intelligentsia overdid its praise once it had discovered Lardner. But whatever else was involved, two basic facts can not be minimized in accounting for the critical acclaim. The first is that the stories Lardner wrote in the decade are generally superior to his earlier ones, not only in technical excellence but also in the range, variety, and depth of subject. The work of his major period thus more fully merited critical accolades than had his earlier work. Second, as the result of his having become thoroughly disenchanted with the American scene by around 1920, there developed in his work a harshly critical tone which was in accord with the intellectual attitude prevailing in the era. Lardner emphatically refused to consider himself an intellectual, and he rebuffed the efforts of those who sought to pin the label on him; but that did not stop the intellectuals from hailing him as a spokesman for the age or from praising his efforts "to get the low-down Americano between covers."[22]

Lardner began writing for the Bell Syndicate in October, 1919, shortly after resigning from the *Tribune* "Wake" column. His new position had the double advantage of bringing him a higher income and of requiring less writing, and it also freed him from the necessity of living in Chicago. He had long desired to be near the New York musical publishing and theatrical center. Thus, in the fall of 1919, he moved his family to Greenwich, Connecticut; he sent three of the children with their nurse by train but drove himself, Ellis, and the other child over by automobile, a trip which supplied the factual basis for *The Young Immigrunts,* one of the most hilarious pieces of humor Lardner ever wrote. He lived in Greenwich only a few months, however, before moving to a large house he had purchased on East Shore Road, Great Neck, Long Island, where he lived for the next seven years.

At Great Neck, Lardner enjoyed as near neighbors not only his brother Rex, his old Niles boyhood friend Arthur Jacks, the columnist Franklin P. Adams, the newspaper editor H. B. Swope, but also Zelda and F. Scott Fitzgerald, with whom he formed a close friendship. In the drinking-partying atmosphere and the very setting made familiar by *The Great Gatsby*—Lardner's house is supposed to have provided Fitzgerald with the inspiration for Gatsby's mansion—Lardner attended big parties, gave parties himself, belonged to clubs, and played bridge and golf. Even though he immediately began satirizing the socialite life of well-to-do, big-city suburbanites (for example, in *The Big Town*, 1921), he apparently quite willingly allowed himself to be drawn into the Long Island "social cesspool," as he regularly referred to it. In this milieu, as in former ones, he was the detached observer and critic; and despite the intimacy which might be expected to develop in all-night drinking and talking sessions with close friends, no one seemed to come to know him well, to see him with his mask off. Fitzgerald, for example, later wrote: "At no time did I feel that I had known him enough, or that anyone knew him—it was not the feeling that there was more stuff in him and that it should come out, it was rather a qualitative difference, it was rather as though, due to some inadequacy in one's self, one had not penetrated to something unsolved, new and unsaid."[23]

According to Edmund Wilson, Lardner did sometimes become loquacious when drunk, but his loquacity might take the form of reading aloud "with a saturnine deadpan scorn" the rule book of the local golf club, or of telling nonsense jokes and fairy tales;[24] or at larger gatherings, it might take the form of improvising "operas" at the piano, such as the one whose heroine, Gretchen, inspired an aria beginning "Oh, Gretchen, I'm retchin' for you."[25]

Lardner was drinking more and more heavily in these years, occasionally going on bouts lasting several weeks. Elder thinks that his heavy drinking resulted from the "deep and ineradicable pessimism" he had developed by this time, which made him "inclined to doubt the value of his very existence" (186-87). But if pessimism was the obvious cause of his heavy drinking, what caused his pessimism? Had it simply grown on him? Was he, despite his huge income, worried about the financial security of his family? Did it result from his frustrated efforts to write songs and shows? Had he lost interest in the kind of writing he was doing successfully so that it had become merely a deadly chore? Had "the blackness of American middle-class life . . . entered into his own soul"?[26]

No one knows the full explanation of Lardner's pessimism, perhaps not even Lardner himself knew it, and certainly no one explanation will entirely account for it. Throughout his married life he was perpetually worried about the comfort and security of his family, a concern he expressed in his heavy subscription to life insurance—the estate of nearly $200,000 he left at his death was composed almost entirely of insurance.[27] He did aspire to write music and shows of the popular Broadway variety; and, though one skit, "The Bull Pen," produced by the Ziegfeld *Follies* in 1922 brought some satisfaction, the repeated frustrations he suffered in his determined efforts to write other things for the *Follies* and to write a play acceptable to George M. Cohan, take on the proportions of a saga. Again and again, he was commissioned to do work which was never produced or, if produced, changed beyond recognition.[28] Only late in the decade, after forming a partnership with George S. Kaufman, did he finally succeed in writing a successful play.

Fitzgerald believed that the ambition to write music and shows caused Lardner to become thoroughly dissatisfied with the kind of writing he was doing successfully, and that by the early 1920's he had developed a cynical attitude toward the work on which his reputation now rests, viewing it as "directionless, merely 'copy'."[29] Earlier, in 1917, Lardner had indicated a desire to change his method of writing: "I'd give anything to be able to stop writing dialect stories. And I'm tired of writing in the first person. I would like to write in the third person."[30] Though he soon began using the third person, he still complained to Edmund Wilson in the Great Neck period that his trouble was that he couldn't write "straight English"—such a sentence, for example, as "We were sitting in the Fitzgeralds' home and the fire was burning brightly."[31] Thus, even if the dissatisfactions with his former achievement and the unhappiness resulting from his apparent inability to switch successfully to different creative veins fail to explain entirely the growth of his pessimistic attitude, they doubtless had a direct bearing on it.

Finally, it must be agreed that the "blackness of American middle-class life . . . had entered his soul." In the blatantly materialistic atmosphere of the postwar 1920's, when the cleavage between an ideal standard of human behavior and the actual standard became wider than ever before, the blackness and blankness of American middle-class life disturbed many other sensitive observers; and Lardner's pessimism was as much the result of the temper of the times as it was of anything else. Yet, in his increasing dissatisfaction with the way things were or with the way he thought they were, it is improbable that he developed as virulent a hatred for society as Clifton Fadiman asserted: "The special force of Ring Lardner's work springs from a single fact: he just doesn't like people. Except Swift, no writer has gone further on hatred alone. I believe he hates himself; more certainly he hates his characters; and most clearly of all, his characters hate each other. Out of this integral triune repulsion is born his icy satiric power."[32] The caustic, sardonic, or coldly furious tone evident in many of his stories of this period does indicate that Lardner intensely disliked and even loathed some of the characters he was writing about, but it was an attitude aroused by particular characters and particular injustices, not by society as a whole or by injustice in the abstract.

In view of the other work which engaged Lardner—his column, the text for the Jack Keefe comic strip, and numerous miscellaneous pieces of humor, satire, and nonsense, as well as his efforts to write for the theater—it is not surprising that his production of stories fell off sharply in the early years of the decade. Besides the five stories making up *The Big Town*—which some critics plausibly classify as a novel rather than as a collection of stories—he wrote only five stories from 1920 to 1925, publishing none at all in either 1923 or 1924. However, three of the five, "Some Like Them Cold," "A Caddy's Diary," and "The Golden Honeymoon" are among his best.

In 1924, under the prompting of Fitzgerald, Lardner published his first collection of separate stories, *How to Write Short Stories* [*With Samples*]. Fitzgerald not only suggested the title for the volume, as well as the burlesque preface and nonsense notes Lardner wrote for it, but he also helped to convince Scribner's to publish it. The inappropriate title and the misleading preface and notes made Edmund Wilson wonder whether the publisher was trying to pass off a serious writer as a humorist or whether Lardner himself was timid about coming forward as a serious writer.[33] Few critics, however, were misled by the comic editorial apparatus, and the book was both a critical and financial success. The reissue by Scribner's soon thereafter of Lardner's earlier books—*You Know Me Al, Gullible's Travels,* and *The Big Town*—gave further solidity to his reputation as a serious writer.

Lardner steadily disparaged his new standing with literary critics: "Where do they get that stuff about me being a satirist? I ain't no satirist. I just listen."[34] But still, acclaim must have given him a new impetus to write stories, for in the four years from 1925 to 1929 he published twenty-seven—all but four of which he deemed worthy of republication either in his next collection, *The Love Nest*, which appeared in 1926, or in *Round Up*, which appeared in 1929. *Round Up* contained thirty-five stories—all of those in *How to Write Short Stories* and *The Love Nest*, plus sixteen others. It is significant that twenty-five of the thirty-five—or over seven-tenths of the stories he himself judged worthy of collecting—were written from 1925 to 1929, clearly the peak years of Lardner's development as a story writer.

The stories of this major period fully display not only the flowering of Lardner's satiric viewpoint but also the height of his technical skill. Finally breaking away from dialect and the first-person narrative method which he had long considered handicaps, he began writing in the third person and using straight English. Though he used characters in many stories who still "maimed and bruised" the English language, he nevertheless wrote a number of stories in which even the dialogue is standard English. Very likely, as Howard Webb has suggested, his satire and his use of the objective third-person are interdependent developments. Whereas the in-character first-person narrator of such works as *Gullible's Travels* and *The Big Town* is a mask for Lardner himself, the use of the third-person allowed him to disassociate himself completely from his characters—that is, to stand outside the range of his own satiric fire and to remain a detached reporter who was in no sense identifiable with his characters.[35]

And the range of his satiric fire was both broad and fierce. It played upon the sadistic practical joker in "Haircut" and "The Maysville Minstrel"; upon the pin-brained, loose-tongued woman in "Zone of Quiet" and "Who Dealt?"; and upon the cruel ego-obsessed show producer in "Love Nest" and "A Day with Conrad Green." It was directed against the proclivity of people to cheat others or themselves in "The Spinning Wheel" and "Mr. Frisbie," against the sheer brutality of prize fighting and the coarse vulgarity of fight fans in "The Venomous Viper of the Volga," and against the hollow asininity of wealthy suburbanites in "High Rollers." It indicted the good old American custom of minding a neighbor's business in "Mr. and Mrs. Fix-It" and "Liberty Hall." Though a few of Lardner's grimmest stories were written in the 'teens and yet other grim ones were to come in the early 1930's, he never before or later displayed the uniformly caustic tone of the stories he wrote from 1925 to 1929.

Nor did Lardner use satire only in his fiction during this period. His other work was miscellaneous in character—parodies, humor, verse, and nonsense plays—but much of it also reflects his deepened critical attitude. It is seen, for example, in an essay he wrote in straight English for Harold E. Stearn's collection *Civilization in the United States, an Inquiry by Thirty Americans* (1922) on "Sport and Play," in which Lardner lashed out against the "anile idolatry" of athletes and contended that the hero-worship of athletes in America was "the national disease that does most to keep the grandstands full and the playgrounds empty" (461). But other subjects besides athletes and their fans drew his attention: such things, for example, as the tendency of a jury to acquit a pretty woman even of murder, the genial host who serves sumptuous dinners and fine liquor to his poker-playing friends while he owes his servant back-wages, the rags-to-riches success story, and so on. Continuing in the vein of satirizing the uplift success story so popular in the magazines of the day, he wrote not only a series of burlesque biographies of prominent people for *Collier's* but also a completely wild nonsense autobiography, *The Story of a Wonder Man* (1927). Though satirizing his own success, this work was not intended as mere self-deprecation, nor were his burlesque biographies meant to be derogatory of their subjects. In both, Lardner was attacking the stereotyped success story, the belief that success results merely from hard work, clean living, and the inspiration supplied by "the little woman."

Regardless of the satire present in his nonfiction, he also continued in it to write in his popular role of humorist and comedian, a role he abandoned altogether in his fiction. While the satirist lurks behind the comic tone of such other works of the period as *Symptoms of Being 35* (1921) and *Say It with Oil* (1923), these are works of humor, not satire; and while satire freely mingles with humor in the collection *What of It?* (1925) that, too, is primarily a work of humor. Finally, the nonsense or "dada" plays he began writing in the early 1920's may be seen representing the "peak of pure hilarity" in his development as a humorist (Elder, 316).

From 1926 on, Lardner's pessimism had another cause—his health. In the summer of that year he discovered that he had tuberculosis and, though the disease was soon brought under control, it recurred. The knowledge of his physical weakness had no immediate effect on his work except to spur him to renewed effort, for now he had a real basis for his concern about the future economic security of his family. He gave up his weekly column in March, 1927, having long been weary of it; but he sorely missed the $30,000 a year it was then bringing him. Thus in 1928, when a collaborative effort with George M. Cohan to produce a play based on his story "Hurry Kane" ended in failure, he again returned to newspaper work, writing four columns a week for the New York *Morning Telegraph* at the reputed salary of $50,000 a year (Elder, 302). Two months after Lardner joined the staff of the *Telegraph* in December, 1928, the paper failed. At last, except for a brief period in 1930 when he again wrote for the Bell Syndicate, he gave up newspaper work entirely. Since 1905, or for the entire twenty-four years of his professional career to that date, he had continuously faced newspaper deadlines, had steadily produced newspaper copy. Probably no other American writer of Lardner's stature remained so long and so closely associated with newspaper work as he.

V   *"That Fine Medallion, All Torn by Sorrow"*

The last four years of Lardner's career (1929-33) involved a prolonged and losing struggle against illness. Along with tuberculosis, he developed heart trouble; and, compelled to spend more and more time in hospitals, he wrote during intervals of intense and determined concentration either at home or in the hospital, as his strength permitted. Working under these circumstances and under the handicap of failing strength, he still managed to produce a sizable quantity of writing, but little of it approached the quality of his earlier work and much of it was mechanical—a reflection of his tremendous effort to turn out marketable copy to the very end.

In 1929 alone, Lardner not only published eight short stories and nineteen magazine articles, but also collaborated with George S. Kaufman in writing *June Moon,* a play adapted from his story "Some Like Them Cold." Tried out first in the summer of 1929 at Atlantic City, the play met a disappointing reception. But Lardner and Kaufman revised it, and when it was produced on Broadway in the fall of 1929, it was highly successful, running for nearly three hundred performances (Elder, 281). In addition to the dozen or so stories he ground out from 1930 on—stories perhaps notable mainly for their compassion, despair, or melancholy–Lardner also wrote another busher series of six stories, published in 1933 as *Lose with a Smile*. The ballplayer on whom the stories focus, Danny Warner, is even more incompetent than Jack Keefe, both in his ballplaying and in his affairs of the heart; and he lacks Jack's bluster and belligerency, getting his feelings hurt, as Jack never would, when another player "sword" (swore at) him.

In the final year and a half of his life, Lardner devoted the major portion of his failing energies to writing a weekly radio column for *The New Yorker* magazine, a work singularly appropriate for him to engage in at that time, not only because of his lifelong interest in music but also because he spent his sleepless nights in the hospital listening to radio shows. He devoted some of the columns to attacking pornographic songs, thereby going on what Fitzgerald called an "odd little crusade,"[36] which drew counterfire from other writers who regarded Lardner as prudish and puritanical. But in matters of sex and obscenity Lardner was a belated Victorian: even in the earlier days, while traveling with ball clubs, he had objected to dirty jokes; and, despite his perpetual concern with domestic relationships in his stories, he completely avoided the issue of sexual relationships (Elder, 358-95). In view of these facts, Elder's description of him as a puritan idealist is justified. Thus, Lardner's little crusade represented no new turn in his thinking; to tell the truth, his objections to suggestive songs were pretty reasonable: he thought it was "silly for radio to bar words like God, Hell, and damn and to permit the 'comedians' to get by with gags running the gamut from vulgar to vile. . . ."[37]

Despite the heavy demands the radio column made on Lardner's failing energies, he also engaged in other work in the final months of his life—notably, another play, planned again as a collaborative effort with Kaufman, but left unfinished at his death. It became increasingly difficult for him to work: Elder says that "he was sometimes found asleep over his typewriter, his forehead bruised from having fallen on the machine" (365); and that "sometimes he was observed alone, with his face in his hands, sobbing" (377). He died at the East Hampton, Long Island, home he had built in 1928 next-door to the Grantland Rices, on September 25, 1933, at the age of forty-eight. In an article written soon after Lardner's death, Fitzgerald described

Lardner as a "proud, shy, solemn, shrewd, polite, brave, kind, merciful, honorable . . ." man and concluded the article by saying: "A great and good American is dead. Let us not obscure him by the flowers, but walk up and look at that fine medallion, all torn by sorrows that perhaps we are not equipped to understand. Ring made no enemies . . . and to many millions he gave release and delight."[38]

VI *Perspectives*

One of the primary facts about Lardner's career as a writer is that he limited himself more strictly than perhaps any other American writer to recording the visible phenomena of his immediate surroundings. "I just listen hard" he repeatedly affirmed; and he reported with artistic impartiality, particularly in his fiction, what he heard and what he saw. He was thus a realist in the nearly perfect sense of the term: without permitting the slightest intrusion of personal feeling, he wrote, not about a world that might be, but entirely about the actual world perceived by his senses.

If there are distortions in his vision of the world, as there probably are, these must be sought in his work itself, for he never recorded—indeed, he appears never to have even spoken—his inner convictions, his personal emotions, except as those may be implied in the objective statement made by his fiction. Whereever one looks for the real Lardner, one comes up solidly against one or another of the masks behind which he so effectively concealed himself: his deadpan demeanor which prevented even close friends from knowing his real feelings, the completely impersonal third person point-of-view of much of his fiction, and the first-person in-character disguise of nearly everything else he wrote. While the in-character disguise is a thin one, often revealing rather than concealing his true convictions, the significant point is that he thereby cast himself in a role; and one can never be certain how fully Lardner used the role to conceal or to reveal his personal convictions.

There was, then, an elusive, enigmatic quality about Lardner's personality, a quality that provoked speculation in his lifetime and provokes it still. After Sherwood Anderson had become acquainted with him in the early 1920's, he wrote: "A long, solemn-faced man. The face was wonderful. It was a mask. All the time, when you were with him, you kept wondering . . . 'What is going on back there?' "[39] Fitzgerald thought that Lardner "had got a habit of silence" during his ballpark days when he had "moved in the company of a few dozen illiterates playing a boy's game," and that the final result of it was that "he had agreed with himself to speak only a small portion of his mind." And in a tone of near-exasperation, Fitzgerald asked, "What did Ring want, how did he want things to be, how did he think things were?"[40] But perhaps Anderson answered his own and Fitzgerald's questions when he said, in a second article he wrote about Lardner, that "there was [in him] something extremely sensitive that did not want to be hurt. . . . He was intent upon covering up, concealing from everyone, at any cost, the shy hungry child he was carrying about within himself."[41] The viewpoint Donald Elder adopts on the issue in his biography of Lardner is in basic agreement with Anderson's—namely, that Lardner was acutely sensitive and that his deadpan expression was a defense against injury. He was a person of principle, a perfectionist, who carried through life with him the idealism he had developed in the "love-locked" family circle of his Niles youth; and his impersonal detachment, his reticence, were coverings worn by a person dismayed by the nonidealistic, topsy-turvy world he observed and recorded in his works.

But though Lardner had a strong attachment to a family tradition, he appeared to have no conscious connection with a literary tradition, even standing apart from the literary movements of his own day. He admired Finley Peter Dunne and George Ade, and they may have exerted some influence on him, but if so, it is hard to discern. He was apparently familiar with the works of Mark Twain, but he displayed erratic taste in regarding Dunne as a better humorist and Booth Tarkington as a better depicter of boys than Mark Twain. Incidental allusions in Lardner's writings show that he had read fairly widely, but there is no evidence that he was intimately acquainted with American literature or with the literature of any other country. It is ironic that he perhaps was totally unaware that his own work was a fusion of two important currents of American literature: first, of the vernacular tradition that began with "Yankee Doodle Dandy" and flowered in the rich mass of humorous writing of the nineteenth century; and second, of the realistic tradition Howells and others were vigorously fighting for in Lardner's youth and which, with a shifting of issues, such writers as Dreiser,

Anderson, and Lewis were still fighting for in Lardner's adulthood.

Lardner, of course, was widely acquainted with the writers of his own day, but again there is no indication that any of them, even Fitzgerald who was long a close friend, exerted any influence on him. He lived in Chicago during the very period that the "robin egg" literary renaissance—as Anderson described it—occurred, a renaissance heralded by a sudden creative outflow from the pens of such writers as Sandburg, Masters, Dell, Hecht, and Anderson himself, whose *Winesburg, Ohio,* appeared in 1919. Yet, if Lardner was even aware at that time of this surge of literary activity or of these writers, he gave no indication of his awareness. And throughout the very period when these and other writers were revolting from the village and had begun to indict village life in their works, Lardner consistently referred to Niles with fondness and nostalgia.

Thus despite the fact that the prevailing tone of Lardner's work fits the literary temper of his age as fully as the work of Dreiser, Anderson, and Lewis does, he traveled his own separate literary path. He was an objective reporter of what he observed, and the result is that his work, stage by stage, springs directly from the American milieu he witnessed. In the complete sense of Howells' dictum, he was as fully American as he unconsciously could be. As Virginia Woolf said: ". . . Mr. Lardner does not waste a moment when he writes in thinking whether he is using American slang or Shakespeare's English; whether he is remembering Fielding or forgetting Fielding; whether he is proud of being American or ashamed of not being Japanese; all his mind is on his story. Hence, incidentally, he writes the best prose that has come our way. Hence we feel at last freely admitted to the society of our fellows."[42]

Lardner's consistent refusal to regard himself as an intellectual or to look upon himself as a serious literary artist may have had its basis not only in modest self-deprecation but also in a deep-seated conviction that he really was *not* a "literary" man but a journalist, as he repeatedly insisted. Certainly the vast quantity of ephemeral writing he did—straight news writing for nine years, newspaper columns for fourteen years, and a mass of magazine articles closely akin to newspaper writing—lends justification to his viewpoint. Further, it is notable that, with only a few minor exceptions, everything that he wrote was first published either in a newspaper or a mass-circulation magazine—the *Saturday Evening Post,* the *Red Book, Cosmopolitan,* the *American, Collier's, Liberty,* and so on. This includes the more than 120 short stories he wrote (counting installments of sequence groups as separate stories); and the fact that he chose to reprint less than half of this total— and even had to be persuaded to reprint some of that half—may indicate that he really regarded his fiction as little more than journalism.

Someone has remarked that a writer deserves to be judged by the best he wrote, not by the worst; and included among the great quantity and variety of Lardner's writing—humor, plays, burlesque biographies, verse, columns, and fiction—there is a solid and substantial body of work which adequately justifies assigning him to a rank of literary importance. The chapters which follow undertake to describe, interpret, and evaluate this body of work.

CHAPTER 2

The Busher Stories

THE FIRST of the twenty-six stories Lardner wrote using rookie baseball pitcher Jack Keefe as the main character appeared in the March 7, 1914, issue of the *Saturday Evening Post*. By coincidence or expert editorial timing, March 7 was the very day that a large group of enthusiastic baseball fans gave the Chicago White Sox and the New York Giants an elaborate banquet to welcome them home from a world tour; they went out in the New York harbor the day before to meet the steamer carrying the teams and escorted it to the docks with a brass band and other fanfare. The tour had carried the teams to such places as Japan, China, the Philippine Islands, Australia, Egypt, Italy, France, and England; and its aim had been to arouse world interest in baseball with the hope of making the game a truly international sport.

Whatever success the trip had enjoyed in foreign eyes—and Comiskey, the White Sox owner, thought all the countries visited except Egypt showed promise of mastering the game—it was widely applauded by the American public who, long converted to the merits of baseball, treated the teams as conquering heroes. The White Sox were given a second banquet in Chicago when they arrived there a few days later, and with the volunteer assistance of countless news writers, cartoonists, and sports fans, Lardner and Edward C. Heeman prepared an elaborately illustrated souvenir booklet to commemorate the homecoming.[1]

Lardner thus launched his busher before a baseball-loving public made even more conscious of the game by the world tour and the publicity attending it. But, though Lardner bowed his hero on stage in a blaze of publicity favorable to baseball, he bowed him off in a harsher glare of unfavorable publicity. For the last of the busher stories appeared October 13, 1919, on the eve of the World Series games of that year, later discovered to have been rigged by gamblers in collusion with White Sox players, who threw the series to the inferior Cincinnati Reds. The resulting scandal shocked the baseball-loving public; but as Gilbert Seldes has remarked, no understanding reader of the Keefe stories should have been shocked.[2] For even the explanation that Eddie Cicotte, the White Sox pitcher, gave of his key role in throwing the series sounded like a remark from the mouth of a Lardner character: "I did it for the wife and kiddies," he said. By 1919, Lardner was ready to abandon Jack Keefe and writing about baseball, but the scandal may have hastened his decision. Apparently, he managed to write the text for the comic-strip revival of Keefe in the early 1920's only by the exercise of sheer will power, and induced by the $17,500 a year which the strip brought him.

Lardner wrote all the Keefe stories for the *Saturday Evening Post*. They appeared in five related groups, as follows:

1. An initial group of six, published from March 7 to November 7, 1914, and republished in book form as *You Know Me Al* in 1916. The best-known group, it clearly merits more recognition than any of the others.

2. A second group of five, published from March 20 to June 5, 1915. These have not been republished, and for convenience in the discussion which follows this group will be referred to as *The Busher Abroad*.

3. A third group of four, published from March 9 to June 8, 1918, three of which were reprinted as *Treat 'Em Rough: Letters from Jack the Kaiser Killer*, 1918. The first of this group, "Call for Mr. Keefe" shows Jack, like other good Americans before and after his time, trying to evade his draft call, a fact which may explain why it was omitted from a book collection appearing in a war year.

4. A fourth group of six, published from July 6, 1918, to January 25, 1919, and republished in 1919 as *The Real Dope*. Since both groups 3 and 4 concern themselves with Jack's army career, they perhaps more properly can be regarded as a single long sequence than as different groups.

5. The final group of five, published from April 19 to October 13, 1919. This group has not been republished and will be referred to as hereafter as *The Busher Re-enlists*.

Over thirteen years after the appearance of the final Jack Keefe story, Lardner once more wrote a group of stories dealing with a busher–one named Danny Warner, a character quite different from Jack Keefe. Six in number, these stories were also published in the *Saturday Evening Post,* from April 23 to September 3, 1932; they were republished as *Lose with a Smile* in 1933, the year Lardner died. This work will be discussed in this chapter because it provides an interesting contrast to the Keefe stories and permits one to see the difference between Lardner's earlier and later treatment of ballplayers.

I *You Know Me Al*

Friend Al: Well old pal I suppose you seen in the paper where I been sold to the White Sox. Believe me Al it comes as a surprise to me and I bet it did to all you good old pals down home. You could of knocked me over with a feather when the old man comes up to me and says Jack I've sold you to the Chicago Americans. . . .

He says we aren't getting what you are worth but I want you to go up to that big league and show those birds that there is a Central League on the map. He says go and pitch the ball you been pitching down here and there won't be nothing to it.[3]

Thus begin the adventures of Lardner's inimitable rookie pitcher in the big league, told through the mounting flow of letters he writes his Bedford, Indiana, hometown pal, Al Blanchard. "I will just give them what I got and if they don't like it they can send me back to the old Central and I will be perfectly satisfied," he assures Al (10). And when he flubs miserably in his initial attempt—disregarding training rules, refusing to take advice, supremely confident of his prowess—he is sent back, not to the Central League, but to the West Coast League. Making a comeback, however, he wins the key game in the city "serious" (series) and has his contract renewed with an increase in salary.

Meanwhile, convinced that the girls find him irresistible, a conviction he never loses, he has been engaging in affairs of the heart: first, with Violet, "real society and a swell dresser" (21), who breaks with him when he is demoted; and then, in San Francisco, with Hazel, "a great big stropping girl that must weigh one hundred and sixty lbs" (48), who is willing to marry him immediately. But Jack puts her off to the end of the season, when he will have more money; and after his successful return to the big league, Violet shows a willingness to resume relations with him, a fact which causes Jack to wish "they was two of me so both of them girls could be happy" (66). Hazel, however, decides to marry a middle-weight prize fighter—"Al . . . she was no good and I was sorry the minute I agreed to marry her" (75)—and Violet throws him over for a left-handed pitcher. Finally, he marries Florence, the sister-in-law of a teammate, writing Al: "She maybe ain't so pretty as Violet and Hazel but as they say beauty isn't only so deep" (81). When he and his new wife, whom he calls Florrie, have their first "quarrle" over his former affairs, he tells her all about Hazel and Violet "except that I turned them down cold at the last minute to marry her," he explained to Al, "because I did not want her to get all swelled up" (88).

Despite Jack's boast to Al that "some men lets their wife run all over them but I am not that kind," Florrie foils his efforts to make her spend the winter in the inexpensive house he has leased in Bedford and instead gets him to take an expensive flat in Chicago into which, to Jack's dismay, also move Florrie's sister and her husband. Dumb, gullible Jack finds himself paying for the flat, buying meals for four persons, and employing a servant to do the housekeeping. When his money runs out, he goes, at Florrie's insistence, not only to seek an advance on his next year's salary but also unreasonably to beard Comiskey for an increase in salary, which is refused. After Florrie walks out in a fit of anger and Comiskey tells him that he is going to be sold to Milwaukee, Jack's affairs appear to be completely on the rocks.

They gradually straighten out, however: he is not sold to Milwaukee, he is reunited with Florrie and becomes the father of a son: "Friend Al. . . . I am the happyest man in the world . . . ." (163). But, when the baby waves his left hand, Jack worries that he will be left-handed and wants to consult a doctor "because they must be some way of fixing babys so as they won't be left handed. And if nessary I will cut his left arm off of him. Of coarse I would not do that Al. But how would I feel if a boy of mine turned out like Allen and Joe Hill and some of them other nuts?" (165). At the end of this sequence of stories Jack is preparing, with trepidation about the safety of boats, to go on the 1913-14 world tour with the White Sox and Giants.

The image of himself that Jack unconsciously presents to Al and the reader is thus the reverse of the one he has of himself.

He regards himself as honest and fair-minded, but he deludes himself and lies to others. He considers himself free of faults, but those he finds in others—stinginess, intemperance, crude behavior, selfishness—are his own. He believes that he is a man of nerve and courage, but he readily finds excuses for not following up his frequent threats to sock somebody in the jaw, sometimes displaying downright cowardice. He thinks he is quick-witted and clever at repartee, but typically the best he can manage is something like this: "He says pretty lucky Boy but I will get you next time. I came right back at him. I says Yes you will" (57). Or when he does better, he laboriously explains the point to Al:

> . . . Hill hollers to me and says I guess this is where I shoot one of them bean balls. I says Go ahead and shoot and if you hit me in the head and I ever find out I will write and tell your wife what happened to you. You see what I was getting at Al. I was insinuateing that if he beaned me with his fast one I would not never know nothing about it if somebody did not tell me because his fast one is not fast enough to hurt nobody even if it should hit them in the head. So I says to him Go ahead and shoot and if you hit me in the head and I ever find out I will write and tell your wife what happened to you. See, Al? (159)

He is sure that he never loses a game because of incompetence; he loses because of the faulty playing of his teammates, the mistakes the umpire makes, the rough ground he stumbles on while fumbling a bunt, and so on. Stupid, gullible, brash, ignorant, supremely self-confident, he bangs and bungles along, failing to learn from experience, disregarding the advice of others, and permitting the same faults to get him into one predicament after another.

The portrait Lardner develops of Keefe in this initial presentation of him satirizes the ballplayer, but the satire reflects a dispassionately ironic mood—not the angry mood evident behind the satire of much of Lardner's later fiction. Jack is an innocent moving in a highly competitive world, and he impotently strives to make this world appreciate his true worth, but it continually rejects his self-created image and perpetually thwarts his best efforts.

While this portrait of a ballplayer debunks the stereotyped image of the athlete as a public idol, Lardner obviously depicts Keefe as an individualized, particular athlete and not as a generalized representative of athletes as a class. Jack Keefe is a definite personality, a specific human being, stumbling around in the shadowy world of his twisted values and faulty perceptions. In this latter sense, Lardner developed him into a character whose significance extends to the larger world outside the ballpark where countless other persons seek bread and status and are beset by the same handicaps that interfere with Jack's struggle to attain them on the ball field. As others have noted,[4] Jack is a universal type who could just as well have been shown struggling in any one of a dozen different occupations: that he is a ballplayer is thus incidental to his larger significance.

Nevertheless, for Lardner the choice of a baseball player as the main character of his first sustained fictional effort was both convenient and inevitable; its soundness, as Virginia Woolf has shown, was based on more than Lardner's intimate familiarity with ballplayers and baseball: "It is no coincidence that the best of Mr. Lardner's stories are about games, for one may guess that Mr. Lardner's interest in games has solved one of the most difficult problems of the American writer; it has given him a clue, a centre, a meeting place for the divers activities of people whom a vast continent isolates, whom no tradition controls. Games give him what society gives his English brother."[5] She might have added—as her statement implies—that games are played by rules, by a code so well known to players and fans alike, that its emblem has become a universal cliché: "It's not who wins or loses that counts, but how you play the game."

The projection of his character against the backdrop of the game and the code governing its playing permitted Lardner to present Jack's lineaments with graphic clarity, a clarity that would have been harder to attain had he been involved in a different kind of game or one played by a code less well known to Lardner's readers than the baseball code. For this reason, it is easy to understand why the ball-fan readers of the *Post* followed the Keefe stories avidly (Lardner was eventually receiving over $1,200 a piece for them): Keefe could be viewed as the very opposite of the ideal ballplayer, and viewed thus he became a comic figure, not a satiric one.

The fact that the Keefe stories, as well as much of Lardner's other fiction, had the appeal of humor to one class of readers and of satire to another, explains not only why he attracted both a popular and a serious literary following in his day but also why he was viewed by the first group as a humorist only and by the second as a social critic. Richard Watts, Jr., explained Lardner's dual appeal as "a remarkable gift for being both funny and savage at the same time, without letting either quality interfere with the other. Jack Keefe . . . is not only obnoxious but prodigiously comic, but the thing about him is that it is not his obnoxiousness which is comic. The fun arises from his fatuous and abysmal ignorance about himself, and thus it is possible for him to be a figure of comedy for one reason and of social criticism for quite another."[6] The comedy of Jack's ignorance of himself is in every page of *You Know Me Al*—in his language, in his consistently unconscious reversals or revisions of ideas and plans, and, above all, in his naïveté, a trait which causes him to report to Al even the insults he receives. Cited, for example, is his report of Comiskey's response to his inquiry about taking Florrie along to the team's spring training camp in California:

> He says Sure they would be glad to have her along. And then I says Would the club pay her fair? He says I guess you must of spent that $100 buying some nerve. He says Have you not got no sisters that would like to go along to? He says Does your wife insist on the drawing room or will she take a lower birth? He says Is my special train good enough for her?
>
> Then he turns away from me and I guess some of the boys must of heard the stuff he pulled because they was laughing when he went away but I did not see nothing to laugh at. But I guess he ment that I would have to pay her fair if she goes along and that is out of the question Al (108).

And this denseness leads him steadily to reveal all his other defects with never a trace of awareness that the light he throws on himself is often pitiless: ". . . I am glad I got a wife with some sense though she kicked because I did not get no room with a bath which would cost me $2 a day instead of $1.50. I says I guess the clubhouse is still open yet and if I want a bath I can go over there and take the shower. She says Yes and I suppose I can go and jump in the lake. But she would not do that Al because the lake here is cold at this time of the year" (84-85).

But Lardner's initial portrait of his ignoramus develops a warmly sympathetic tone. It is particularly evident in the scene where Jack returns to his apartment to find that Florrie has walked out on him and in the scenes where Jack is presented as the insanely proud parent, worried that little Al has the "collect" (colic) or that the "train" nurse is neglecting him. The ironic refrain "You Know Me Al" runs through the book as a reminder that Jack holds a false image of himself, but that refrain is counterbalanced by the equally persistent cry for sympathy: "Al, I am up against it again." Being what he is, Jack is doomed eternally to be up against it, so that the underdog role he play evokes both laughter and sighs, as Lardner clearly intended it to.

II *The Busher Abroad*

In the last installment of *You Know Me Al*, Lardner's busher is preparing to join the Chicago White Sox and New York Giants on the international tour they made to popularize baseball in other countries. The journey itself, the exhibition games played under varying circumstances, and the events occurring aboard ship provide the substance of the five stories making up *The Busher Abroad* sequence, a work decidedly inferior to *You Know Me Al*. For having committed his character to the framework of a trip actually made, having taken him away from the drama of his domestic relationships, and being also obliged to show him playing in games where nothing is really at stake, Lardner deprived himself of some of the resources which gave pungency to *You Know Me Al*. Nevertheless, *The Busher Abroad* is not totally lacking in interest and appeal.

The Busher Abroad, more strictly than *You Know Me Al,* is a work of humor; and although the international setting might have afforded Lardner almost unlimited possibilities for different types of humor, the chief—nearly the sole—source of it is the underdog-ignoramous role his busher plays. The stories center almost entirely on Jack's stupidity in accepting at face value the wild tales his more imaginative companions tell him and in permitting himself to be the dupe of their countless practical jokes.

In "Honk Honk" (Hong Kong), for example, they tell him that Orientals eat only rat meat, which can afflict them with "hiderofobeya" and make them think they are rats. Jack refuses to eat anywhere but on shipboard, and when the ship leaves China headed for "Vanilla" (Manilla) in the "Philip Bean Illands" and Jack is told that a teammate is headed for his stateroom squeaking like a rat and looking for cheese, he bolts the door and cowers with fright. When the ship is sailing around the Australian coast, his teammates convince him that the "Australian bite" (bight) is a huge bird with an animal-like head which swoops down on ships and bites off the facial features of passengers who expose themselves on deck, that it can chew its way through screen and wood but not through a catcher's mask. Finding all the masks already reserved for the players who are preparing to stand on deck and fight off the menace with baseball bats, Jack stays below deck in his "birthroom" for three days until the ship is out of the danger zone; but he is soon again frightened by tales of a supposedly equally dangerous "Thomas Hawk" bird which inhabits the Indian Ocean. When the ship reaches the equatorial line, his comrades inform him that the ship will have to climb an elevation; so Jack manfully pulls on a rope tied to the front of the ship to help lift it over the elevation and boasts to Al that he played a decisive role in the feat. They get him terribly confused about the international dateline, where a day is gained, by pointing out that he will be separated from Florrie one day less than she will be from him. At Christmas, they present Jack with a neatly gift-wrapped package containing his own dirty, grease-spotted dress shirt which he has been too stingy to have cleaned—and so on. Jack's incredible stupidity, coarse manners, and gullibility are the consistent focus of the humor.

Unlike *You Know Me Al,* where the minor characters lend depth, verisimilitude, and color to the narrative, the minor characters in *The Busher Abroad* are seldom more than shadowy, background figures. Given the framework of the stories, most of them were actual, well-known ballplayers, a fact which may have imposed a restraint on Lardner's treatment of them. Yet he had also used living players in *You Know Me Al*; and he made Casey Stengel one of the most interesting and realistic characters in his much later busher group, *Lose with a Smile.* The likelier explanation is that Lardner, having placed his characters in a habitat he was acquainted with only by hearsay, was reduced to showing them engaged most constantly in doing the one thing he could be certain from his prior knowledge they would be doing—playing jokes on a dumb teammate.

At its best and brightest, the quality of humor in *The Busher Abroad* approaches that of Mark Twain's *Innocents Abroad;* but it never equals the humor of that work, and much of it is pretty thin, bordering on pure absurdity. Moreover, the consistent focus on Jack's unlimited credulity, giving him a largely passive role and no means of getting back at his tormentors as he sometimes does in *You Know Me Al,* becomes tiresome. Lardner's vernacular style lends verve and color to the work, but as a whole it is the least worthy of the five groups of Keefe stories.

III *Treat 'Em Rough and The Real Dope*

Again centered on Jack's credulity and presenting him for a second time in an unfamiliar setting, the ten stories forming *Treat 'Em Rough* and *The Real Dope* share the inherent defects of *The Busher Abroad* group. Still, the placing of the character in an army setting—first in an American training camp, then in an overseas camp, and finally in front-line trenches—gave much broader scope to Lardner's inventive powers. While Jack is the constant target of practical jokesters, he is not so passive as in *The Busher Abroad;* he strikes back with crude jokes of his own or at least with threats of violence; and as in *You Know Me Al,* but not in *The Busher Abroad,* he frequently deserves the rough treatment his comrades give him. Moreover, the two group of stories display a richly varied assortment of minor characters—privates, non-coms, officers, wives, girl friends, and the like—and these, together with the range of comic situations the army setting made possible, permitted Lardner to display again, as in *You Know Me Al,* all of his busher's traits, not merely his stupidity.

If Lardner was under any handicap in showing Keefe playing a soldier's role, in depicting the other soldiers of a wartime American civilian army, or in coping with the more technical details of army routine, it is not visible in either group of stories. He had gained some insight into rear-zone phases of army life and a little knowledge of the psychological outlook of soldiers during the brief trip he made to France in 1917 as a war correspondent for *Collier's,* but hardly enough to account for the authenticity of the war background of *Treat 'Em Rough* and *The Real Dope,* which must be credited, evidently, to his habit of "listening hard."

Nevertheless, the presentation of an already fully defined, nondeveloping character on such a scale, at such great length, resulted in Lardner's inability to do more than vary the comic situations and minor characters and permit Jack to exhibit over and over again his same old bundle of obnoxious traits. By 1918, Lardner's busher had become a stereotyped character, and even though some interest was gained by the minor characters and the attraction of good comic scenes, these two groups of stories lack the freshness and vitality of *You Know Me Al.* Still, one would not go so far as to accept Gilbert Seldes's accusation that the stories of *Treat 'Em Rough* and *The Real Dope* "degenerate into a series of far-fetched practical jokes."[7] They are much more than that, and one even wonders whether, had he read them before reading *You Know Me Al,* he would not have found them as freshly appealing as the earlier work.

The leading plot lines of these stories can be quickly summarized. Swinging into the baseball season in 1918, after the sinking of the "Louisiana" and the declaration of war against Germany, Jack gets a deferment on a draft call because of the two dependents he has to "sport." But someone gives his draft board the tip that Florrie has opened a beauty shop which is bringing in enough to support her and little Al adequately; so Jack is called to the colors, boasting to Al as he goes of his newly discovered enthusiasm to become a Kaiser killer. At Camp Grant, where he is sent for basic training, Jack soon trembles for his life because a practical joker convinces him that the man in the bunk on one side of him is "Nick, The Blade," who is planning to knife him at the first opportunity, and that the man in the bunk on the other side, who keeps asking the Lord, "Do you want me to kill?" may get a positive answer any moment. But Nick turns out to be one of Jack's baseball fans, and the other man, a conscientious objector; so Jack survives and is even promoted to corporal.

Meanwhile, finding the name and address of a lonesome lady in Texas in a pair of Red Cross socks he receives, Jack begins corresponding with her. When he is sent to a camp in Texas, he arranges to meet her under the clock in a Houston hotel lobby. It develops that she is an unattractive, thirty-five-year-old woman—"a woman her age should ought to know more then start writeing letters to a guy she never seen"—and Jack claims to be somebody else until an old baseball buddy comes up and says "Well if here ain't old Jack Keefe."[8] The sudden intrusion of Florrie and little Al, who are paying him a surprise visit, rescues him from his predicament. But overseas he continues his attempted philandering, this time with a Red Cross girl who delivers to Jack's sergeant a crude, sentimental Valentine poem Jack has written her. At the conclusion of a self-laudatory address on baseball Jack makes to the soldiers of his company, the sergeant reads the Valentine poem aloud for the edification of Jack's comrades.

The peak of the humor, however, is reached in the "Stragety and Tragedy" installment (Chapter III) of *The Real Dope.* After Jack writes for his regimental newspaper an article entitled "War and Baseball 2 Games where Brains Wins," pointing out that smart playing wins in both cases and that the army would be much better off if its generals ". . . had of played baseball in the big leagues and learned to think quick,"[9] he is invited in a letter purporting to be from "Black Jack Pershing" to supply the General Staff with some of his strategically valuable baseball secrets. But the big secret, it develops, is that war and baseball are not alike: for Jack points out that opposing ball teams have the same number of players, but that one general can use more men than the opposing general; that games begin at specified times, whereas one general can get the jump on the other by beginning the battle at an unspecified time, and so on. The "Tragedy" part of the title refers to Jack's being caught by a French father in the act of stooping down to kiss his pretty daughter and his having to flee after mollifying the indignant father with a "20 franks" note.

In the final outcome of the series of stories, Jack crawls out between the American and German trenches searching for a lost comrade who is even dumber than he is: grappling there in the darkness with a soldier he takes to be a German, but who is really one of his own comrades also searching for the lost soldier, Jack is wounded in the arm by cross fire. Sent to a hospital, he attempts a one-arm courtship of an army nurse, despite having just received the news that Florrie has presented him with a baby girl. In the end, he is sent home to assist in the liberty loan drive.

Even when it is fully acknowledged that much of the humor of *Treat 'Em Rough* and *The Real Dope* has a contrived quality, reflecting the pressure Lardner was under in continuing to invent new situations to place his interminable busher in, these works nevertheless deserve a higher ranking than *The Busher Abroad.*

IV *The Busher Re-enlists*

The final group of five stories Lardner wrote about busher Keefe picks up where *The Real Dope* left off: with the busher's return to the United States and his subsequent discharge from the army. Not wanting to return to baseball, now that "all games seems like baby games after what I went through acrost the old pond," Jack seeks other employment, but without success. He tells Al: ". . . this is a fine burgh where a lot of the business men don't know they's been a war or read papers or nothing only set in front of the cash register and watch how the money rolls in or else they must of bet 20 cents on the Kaiser and have got a gruge against the boys that stopped him."[10]

Compelled to return to the only profession he knows, he rejoins the White Sox, who feel obliged to take him back because of his war service. Thus he resumes a baseball career from neither his own free choice nor the team manager's, a fact which means that in the *Busher Re-enlists,* Lardner places his character under dramatic tensions as great as those of *You Know Me Al.* The character's fate is even more dangerously and immediately dependent at every turn on his behavior.

Lardner enhances the gravity of the busher's situation still further by having Florrie sell her thriving beauty shop and take an ill-advised plunge into a partnership arrangement which fails. Florrie loses money and quits work, leaving Jack solely responsible for supporting his family on a lower salary than he was getting before his army service. Lardner thus shows the busher struggling against even harsher economic reality than ever before, where heavy stakes ride on the kind of ball playing Keefe does. Under the persistent surveillance of manager Kid Gleason, who takes Jack's whiskey away from him as often as he catches him with it, who heads off his attempted extra-marital affairs when he can, and who tries to patch up Jack's quarrels with Florrie, the busher plays well; but only in spurts. For his old failings steadily hound him, except that now they take a more extreme form: he drinks more heavily than before; his domestic affairs are rockier and more seriously affect his playing; more quickly provoked to anger than before, his temper tantrums continue for weeks at a time; and his attentions to other women reach such a fatuous peak that on one occasion, with Florrie sitting at his side, he secretly holds the hand of a girl he thinks is lovesick for him.

In this tough situation, as the money Florrie has saved up steadily dwindles away, Jack increasingly permits his vices to impede his playing, so that he becomes a liability to the White Sox; and when he walks off the playing field in a fit of temper one day, they sell him to the Philadelphia Athletics, an inferior team. Though Jack vows never to play for the Athletics, he and Florrie are now down to their last $200, and at the end Jack is on his way to join the new team, predicting that the White Sox will lose the World Series that year. In placing that prophecy in the mouth of the busher and removing him from the White Sox team when he did, Lardner could not have foreseen the scandal of that year's World Series, which changed the name of the White Sox to the "Black Sox."

In this final presentation of his epically drawn but non-epic character, Lardner nevertheless depicts Keefe on a downward course of development. Keefe does not fall into the trap of bribery that his real-life White Sox counterparts did, but he is utterly incapable of releasing himself from the trap he has been in from the beginning—that of his own egocentric ignorance. As his circumstances worsen and his vices become more extreme, the trap tightens. Despite the occasional flashes of insight Keefe shows in *The Busher Re-enlists* group, such as his not wanting to return to baseball or strongly advising Florrie not to sell her shop, Lardner would have been guilty of presenting the busher out of character had he shown him acknowledging defeat or even fully recognizing it. In the final glimpse of him he is swaggering off to try again, spewing out boasts and threats in his customary manner; he is the same old vain braggart he has been ever since his first appearance in *You Know Me Al.* Thus, despite the minor changes in Keefe that Lardner displayed as he concluded his massive treatment of the character —placed between one set of covers the Keefe stories would make a book about the size of *Don Quixote,* if not larger—the busher remains to the end basically a static character whose troubles deepen but whose characteristics remain unaltered. If the *Busher Re-enlists* contributes little new to the reader's knowledge of Keefe's character, the work nevertheless has an appeal and color, a dramatic quality nowhere else so fully displayed in the Keefe stories except in *You Know Me Al;* next to it *The Busher Re-enlists* deserves recognition.

V *Lose With A Smile*

For over thirteen years following the publication of the last group of Jack Keefe stories—the period during which Lardner reached the peak of his career—he turned to other types of characters and produced only a few stories centered on athletes or sports of any kind and only two about baseball. In these years important changes occurred in Lardner's interests and viewpoints so that, as might be expected, his later treatment of a busher in *Lose with a Smile,* which appeared in 1932, is quite different from his treatment of him in the Keefe groups. The question of why Lardner in the last year and a half of his life decided to return to his earliest subject matter may have no certain answer. Still, it is noteworthy that in the winter of 1931-32, just before the six stories forming the *Lose with a Smile* group began appearing in the *Saturday Evening Post,* Lardner wrote—also for the same magazine—a series of rather nostalgic autobiographical sketches about his early baseball-reporter days, recalling many of the colorful and eccentric players he had encountered. Possibly the writing of these sketches revived his interest in doing more stories about baseball very much as the writing of *Life on the Mississippi* had served to stir Mark Twain's recollection of his earlier days and stimulated him to write fiction with a Mississippi River setting.

In the smaller, less important orbit of Lardner's career, however, *Lose with a Smile* hardly holds the place that *Tom Sawyer* or *Huckleberry Finn* holds in Twain's. For despite the expertness of its craftsmanship, it is the work of a writer whose creative energies are fading, and the cheerful nostalgia of the autobiographical sketches is totally absent from its pages: rather its tone is that of hopelessness and despair. Gilbert Seldes has said of *Lose with a Smile* that ". . . when Lardner reverted to his first theme, his heart was not engaged. He was no longer amused, and the book may be funny, but it is not amusing. It is melancholy."[11] The melancholy effect of the work, however, may be due not so much to Lardner's disengagement of heart as to the bleakness and resignation of his mood at the time he wrote it.

The stories focus on the futile efforts of a rookie outfielder, Danny Warner, to make good with the Brooklyn team so that he can afford to marry his Centralia, Illinois, hometown sweetheart, Jessie Graham. The stories are narrated through a series of letters exchanged between the two characters; so that instead of a single dominant character there are two main characters, and the primary focus rests on their relationship rather than on Danny's ballplaying. As a character, Danny bears some resemblance to Jack Keefe: he is dumb, he misses the irony his team managers direct at him, he has girl troubles, he breaks a few training regulations, he boasts now and then, and once he gets put out of a game for talking back to the umpire. But regardless of his possession of such traits, Danny's resemblance to Jack is very superficial.

For one thing, Lardner presented Keefe as a player who could succeed whenever he held his vices in check and really tried; Danny is simply a poor player, a bench-warmer occasionally called on to serve as a pinch-hitter, but of such limited capacity as to make it doubtful that he can succeed at ballplaying or anything else. For another, Jack customarily obeyed instructions only under duress; Danny obeys willingly enough on most occasions, listening to advice and trying to learn, though too pathetically limited to learn. For a third, Jack typically displayed an attitude of animosity or jealousy toward his teammates; Danny is glad to see a teammate make a good showing, even when he and the other player are competing for the same position. In contrast to Jack, Danny is so softhearted that he lets himself be tagged out on a base-steal rather than risk spiking an opposing player; and when told, finally, that he is being farmed out to the Jersey City minor league team, he goes to his room "and lade down on the bed and cride like . . . a baby" (168). In short, Danny is a helpless character; he gives in to defeat without making a serious effort to avoid it.

Danny's love life matches his ballplaying. When he has a blind date with the sister-in-law of a teammate, she turns out to be a predatory gold-digger who makes him spend $42.00 on food, drinks, and tips at a fancy dining place. A Florida telephone girl, with whom he has had a date or two, follows him to Brooklyn and tries to make him responsible for getting her a job, in the meanwhile causing him to pour out his meager funds on food and drink, as the other girl had. These affairs, which he fully reports to his real sweetheart Jessie, affect their relationship of course, but never to the point of breaking it off; for Jessie is just the simple-minded, sweet soul Danny is. At the end, Danny and Jessie's relationship comes to this complete impasse: Danny has decided not to go to the Jersey City team but to wander around New York City looking for work as a "grooner" (crooner), even though his talent for singing is even less promising than his talent for ballplaying. His letter carrying this news to Jessie crosses in the mails one from her telling him that she is coming to visit relatives in Jersey City and wants Danny to meet her at the Penn station "as I will be scared to death if you don't" (174). And the last story ends there, leaving the reader to wonder whether the two are destined ever to meet again or to wander along separate, aimless, meaningless paths thereafter.

Perhaps the most interesting character in the book is Casey Stengel, whom Lardner makes the roommate, friend, and caretaker of Danny. As coach of the Brooklyn team in 1932, Stengel had not yet gained the national fame that came later; but Lardner presented him as true to life—a person with a warm heart concealed behind the rapier-like wit later known as "Stengelese." By having Danny report in his letters to Jessie the well-intended but ironic remarks Stengel made to him, as well as the less well-intended remarks Stengel made to fans and others, Lardner had Danny play a Boswellian role to Stengel. But Stengel's kind, sympathetic treatment of poor Danny is yet another mark of difference between Lardner's earlier and later depiction of baseball and baseball players. Lardner even shows Stengel encouraging Danny in his "grooning" and song-writing efforts, and it is from one of the songs that Danny writes, in imitation of "Life is Just a Bowl of Cherries"–"Life is just a game of baseball so win or lose with a smile"—that the book takes its name.

Significantly, Lardner omitted the "win" part of the song, for with the exception of Stengel, who as a real person must be placed in a different category, the main characters of this book usually lose—but with tears instead of smiles. *Lose with a Smile* is thus no warmed-over *You Know Me Al,* but a totally different work, done in a different tone, and reflecting more sheer pessimism than satire or humor, a pessimism that even carries over into Danny's malapropisms, a point to be developed in the following discussion of Lardner's style.

VI *Style, Structure, and Significance*

Insofar as narrative method alone is concerned, Lardner's busher stories can lay no claim to originality, for the use of the epistolary technique enabling a fictional character not only to tell his story but also reveal the workings of his mind through the letters he writes is at least as old as Samuel Richardson's *Pamela.* It will be remembered that Richardson hit upon the method naturally, as the result of the experience he had acquired in writing letters for the actual counterparts of Pamela. And so it was with Lardner, who had not only served as a letter-writing "secretary" for a real-life counterpart of Jack Keefe,[12] but had also composed letters, purporting to be written by athletes, for his *Tribune* "Wake" column. Thus, when he began the busher stories he was well acquainted with the merit of the epistolary technique and was practiced in its use. Besides his familiarity with the technique and his full awareness of the varied possibilities it afforded for humor, irony, and satire, Lardner probably resorted to it for yet another reason: it permitted him to mask his own viewpoint and remain the impersonal author as well as to unmask the crudely operating mind of the busher. His use of the letter form in the busher was therefore both logical and natural.

By making the letter-writer—narrator a semiliterate busher, Lardner obviously committed himself to write as the busher would write—to fashion the kind of sentences Lardner knew the living prototype of Jack Keefe would fashion, to misspell as he would, to use deformed grammar, distorted syntax, malapropisms, and so on. Lardner's complete mastery of this brand of Americanese, which has been dubbed Lardner "Ringlish" and praised for its accuracy by every critic who has considered it, is clearly one of the primary assets of the busher stories—not simply because it shows how thoroughly Lardner did "listen hard," but rather because it fully expresses the busher's character. For it is through Jack Keefe's onslaught on language that Lardner projects his onslaught on life and lets him draw his own image: "His grammar and syntax . . . are to his folly as genius is to talent.

He cuts the knots of language as if there had never been such a thing as a grammarian. Since he is writing, not talking, he permits himself some formalities and he is forced to spell out what in speech he would mumble without much sense of individual words; but he takes the shortest cut between his meaning and his expression."[13]

Jack, for example, is totally unaware of what can happen to the meaning of a sentence when he simply misplaces a single adverb, as in "She smiled at me and I smiled at her back," or when he combines a misplaced modifier with other deficiences, as in telling Al of his effort to be friendly to his old girl friend and her new husband: "I went over [to their table] because they was no use being nasty and let bygones be bygones." Yet Jack can also communicate his idea unmistakably even across a whole row of double negatives: "We had not did no more scoreing off of Pierce not because he had no stuff but because our club could not take a ball in there hands and hit it out of the infield" (*YKMA*, 192). He can combine the double negative with improper verb forms and still come through clearly: "If I had of thought at the time I would of knew that Detroit never would give no wavers on me after the way I showed Cobb and Crawford up last fall and I might of knew too that Detroit is in the market for good pitchers because they got a rotten pitching staff but they won't have no rotten pitching staff when I get with them" (*YKMA*, 123). And though Jack would have had no better notion of what is wrong with the following sentence than he had of what was wrong with his hitting, its meaning is plainly evident: "Then I swung and missed a curve that I don't see how I missed it" (*YKMA*, 153).

The inherent danger of such an in-character narrative method is that it can force an author to carry the language deformities, particularly the misspellings, to an extreme point where they either obscure the meaning or become tiresome to the reader, as do G. W. Harris' misspellings in the Sut Lovingood yarns. Lardner's certain knowledge of ballplayers, however, enabled him, if not to avoid this danger completely, at least to minimize it. He knew from experience that a ballplayer possessing Jack's language difficulties would seek aid in spelling difficult words, and so Lardner has Jack spell correctly personal and place names which would have been far beyond his range: Comiskey, Callahan, Philadelphia, Cincinnati, and so on.[14] Even though Lardner did not follow this scheme consistently in all the busher stories—Jack sometimes gives unconsciously humorous phonetic renderings of foreign place names—it permitted him to reduce the quantity of the spelling errors.

Conversely, Lardner knew that his illiterate ballplayer would be able to spell common words more easily but would think that he could spell them more accurately than he really could and so would trip over tricky common words that could be easily spelled by even the average baseball fan or reader, who was thus made to feel superior to Jack. True to this pattern, Jack fails to drop the *e* when forming present participles, as in *writeing* and *haveing;* he often drops a vowel from his words, as in *ernest* and *recrut;* and he gets confused between c's and s's, as in *appresiated.* With equal consistency Jack runs aground on phonetic similarity, spelling *piece* as *peace, series* as *serious, whole* as *hole,* and *pain* as *pane.* The incongruity of the unwitting misuse of a word correctly spelled but entirely different from the one intended contributes to the humorous effect at the same time that it keeps the reader reminded that Jack is as far from fulfilling his language intentions as he is from realizing his athletic ones.

In Lardner's last busher group, *Lose with a Smile,* it appears, however, that this type of language incongruity produces a double effect—a humorous one at first glance but on second thought a quite different one which contributes to the bleak tone of that work. Lardner, for example, has Danny write Jessie that he runs like a "street" instead of like a streak, that another player "sword him and called him names" instead of swore at him and called him names, and that a woman cooks in her small apartment at a stove behind a "scream" instead of a screen, and so on. Words as suggestive as these do not occur with enough frequency in *Lose with a Smile* to permit one to say that Lardner consciously reinforced the bleak tone of the work with depressive imagery, but the symbolic or suggestive force of such imagery is nevertheless present and felt. In the sense that a street has no control over where it runs, so Danny had no real control over the course he followed; the sword image perfectly describes how the opposing player's remarks had cut Danny, and the scream image seems highly expressive of the mood a woman conceivably might be in as she cooks in an improvised kitchen.

Returning, however, to the richer vitality of the earlier Keefe stories, one finds that the language deformities follow definable patterns which are seldom out of character or the result of mere whimsicality, a fact which is not surprising since by every report Lardner was painfully meticulous on matters of style. Still, he followed no fixed, consistently unvaried system of language errors throughout the five Keefe groups; sometimes he even showed Jack in one installment of the same group having more difficulty with his syntax than in another—as may be seen, for example, in a comparison of chapters I and III of *You Know Me Al*—or he allowed him to spell words correctly in one story which he misspells in another. Such inconsistencies are credible, for just as the law of averages operated in Jack's pitching, so did it logically function in his spelling.

The element which unifies and controls Lardner's style, however, in his sentence cadence, for he caught to perfection the kind of basic rhythm which is invariably and fundamentally characteristic of folk language. Expressed through the arrangement of word groups within sentences and through the order of sentence units themselves, this rhythmical movement pulls the reader over the cruelest language distortions imaginable, establishes the basic harmony of the style, and lifts Lardner's use of Americanese into the realm of true art. Lardner typically secures this cadence by pruning away excessive modifiers and by reinforcing parallel structure with word repetition, as in the following: "But when I come in Al they was nobody there. They was not nothing there except the furniture and a few of my things scattered round. I sit down for a few minutes because I guess I must of had to much to drink but finally I seen a note on the table addressed to me and I seen it was in Florrie's writing" (*YKMA*, 120). Lardner applied the same principles to the passages of dialogue Jack reports. Hemingway could have gained insight into the handling of dialogue by reading such a typical passage as this: "He says Are you in shape? And I told him Yes I am. He says Yes you look in shape like a barrel. I says They is not no fat on me and if I am a little bigger than last year it is because my mussels is bigger. He says Yes your stumach mussels is emense and you must of gave them plenty of exercise" (*YKMA*, 134). Though such examples are not found on every page of the twenty-six busher stories, they nevertheless are representative passages which illustrate the general quality of the style of the stories. Perhaps more than anything else, it is Lardner's mastery of style, not simply in the busher stories but in his others as well, which enabled him to pull himself above the rank of journalist to the position of a serious literary artist.

Other structural features of the busher stories, however, merit less praise than does Lardner's style. One weakness is that the separate installments of each group are neither fully self-contained short stories nor interdependent parts of a novel. If considered separately, they lose significance; if considered as a sequential group, they fail to display the progressive development of situations and characters which gives sustained appeal to the novel. It may be argued, of course, that a series of short stories centered on a common main character and arranged in a related group permits an author to secure some of the advantages of a novel—familiarity with the characters, general knowledge of the basic situation, sustained suspense—and yet to retain some of the advantages of separate short stories, such as the final and immediate resolution of a tense situation, which permits the reader to relax and start over again without the necessity of remembering all that has gone before. If it is agreed that sequence groups combine such advantages, the busher stories have them; but the inescapable drawback of the method is that it invites the author—indeed, nearly requires him—to treat his character statically, so that he remains from beginning to end basically unchanged, as is true of Jack Keefe and Danny Warner.

A static character can be compellingly interesting, but the amount of interest he can continue to stimulate in the reader bears a relationship to the scale of the author's treatment of him. When an unchanging character is presented on the saga-like scale of Jack Keefe, he is likely to lose the reader's interest after awhile, for the author is reduced simply to inventing different situations and to permitting his character to exhibit the same traits over and over again. For this reason, the structural parallel that Carl Van Doren drew between the busher stories and the comic strip, "wherein a set of personages of established and unchanging characteristics daily meet with mishaps for the amusement of the populace,"[15] is a reasonably accurate one.

Whatever their drawbacks, the busher stories are thoroughly and distinctly in the native American tradition. They could have been produced only by an author with the background and talent Lardner possessed—only by a writer who had so thoroughly observed and been so intimately associated with peculiarly

American phases of life as Lardner had been. Only America could have produced a character like Jack Keefe, and only in America can the peculiar idiom he spoke be found. Finally, the looseness of structure is also in the native American tradition; it is a quality that John A. Kouwenhoven has identified as a common characteristic of such diverse but distinctly American artifacts as the gridiron town plan, the skyscraper, jazz music, Mark Twain's *Huckleberry Finn*, and Walt Whitman's *Leaves Of Grass*. The reason this is so, according to Kouwenhoven, is that all of these artifacts, while laid out on a definite pattern, are composed of "simple and infinitely repeatable units,"[16] a fact which means that the subtraction or addition of units does not fatally alter the basic structure. Lardner obviously could have carried Jack Keefe through additional adventures; but as it is the twenty-six stories he wrote around Keefe make him by far the most fully presented character in Lardner's entire gallery. Despite the interest and the significance of other characters Lardner created, Jack Keefe remains, and will continue to remain, Lardner's fundamentally most important character type.

CHAPTER 3

Gross, Gullible, and Finch

BESIDES the Keefe stories and *Lose with a Smile*, Lardner wrote three other groups of connected stories. Chronologically, the first was a group of seven published in *Redbook* from January, 1915, to May, 1917; in this series Fred Gross, a Chicago police detective, is the main character. Four of these appeared in *Own Your Own Home* (1919), but the other three have not been reprinted. The second group of five stories—appearing in *The Saturday Evening Post* from February 19, 1916, to January 13, 1917—featured an unnamed "Wise Boob" as its main character. These were republished as *Gullible's Travels, Etc.* (1917). The third group—five stories published in *The Saturday Evening Post*, from March 27, 1920, to May 14, 1921—dealt with an ex-cigar salesman named Tom Finch, a boob even wiser than Gullible of *Gullible's Travels*. These reappeared as *The Big Town* (1921).

Fred Gross of *Own Your Own Home* is a variation of the basic character type represented by Jack Keefe; Gullible of *Gullible's Travels* and Finch of *The Big Town* are also variations of one character type, though a type quite different from that depicted in Gross and Keefe. For this reason, it might be said that Lardner introduced only one entirely new major character in these three groups of stories—the "wise boob" represented by Gullible and Finch. To bracket Keefe and Gross on the one hand and Gullible and Finch on the other as character twins, however, is to overemphasize their similarities and slight their differences: Gross is more low-brow than Keefe, and Finch is smarter than Gullible. In stupidity and vulgarity Gross holds the lowest rank among the four, and in intelligence Finch holds the highest, but Gullible ranks between Keefe and Finch, sharing the former's gullibility and the latter's intelligence. Thus, important differences not only distinguish one pair of characters from the other but also each member of the pair from the other, and the recognition of these differences leads to a clearer understanding of what each character represents.

Besides the new major characters depicted in these works, Lardner also added many new minor ones to his fictional gallery. In fact, by the time he finished writing *The Big Town* in 1921, he had presented a fleeting glimpse if not a full portrait of nearly every type representative of middle-class American life of the period and had introduced most of the character types he would use in later fiction.

I Own Your Own Home

Fred Gross of *Own Your Own Home* shares with Jack Keefe such characteristics as stupidity, near-illiteracy, utter naïveté, and supreme self-confidence, and like Jack, he has a total ignorance of his own defects; like him, he tells his troubles and adventures through letters, not to a hometown friend, but to his brother Charley, who lives in another city. But while Jack was crude and coarse, lacking manners, politeness, and courtesy, Fred Gross has even less refinement, and the prominence of these traits in his makeup differentiates him from Jack Keefe. Lardner's choice of the name *Gross* for the character could not have been accidental, because that word, implying mass or bulk as well as lack of finish, keynotes the character's personality. As fond of food and beer as Keefe but with fewer restrictions placed on his eating and drinking habits, Gross is fat and piggish; and the grossness of his physical bulk is more than matched by the rudeness of his behavior. It is expressed most often in his ill-tempered criticism of his wife but most fully in the coarse practical jokes he plays on others in his efforts to avenge imagined wrongs.

The contrast between the basic situations in which the two characters are placed and between their hopes and aims is even more fundamental than the contrast between their personalities. Gross is not involved in a struggle to make good as a policeman: as assistant chief of detectives in the Chicago police department, he is securely established in his profession and on good terms with his superiors, who apparently are no brighter than he. Moreover, whereas in three of the Keefe groups and in *Lose with a Smile* baseball is always the immediate focal point of the action or else provides the backdrop against which it occurs, police work has no parallel significance in the Gross stories but merely serves the purpose of connecting Gross with an occupation in keeping with his characteristics. By contrast, the action of the Gross stories centers almost entirely on his and his wife's attempts to gain social acceptance in the Chicago suburban community of Allison, "16 miles west of the loop," into which they move after building a new home there.

The desire to escape the cramped space of a city apartment and to prevent their children from playing with the hoodlums on city streets motivates the Grosses to move to the suburbs. After surmounting prolonged difficulties in having a house constructed, they occupy it, but find they miss their Chicago friends and set about to make new ones. Rebuffed coldly by their socially elite neighbors, the Hamiltons, they develop a circle of beer-drinking, card-playing friends among the less prominent members of the community; but Gross remains incensed about his inability to gain entry to the community's upper social level. When Gross suddenly becomes the target of crude practical jokes—black crepe paper hung on his door to drive guests silently away from a party, firemen responding to a false alarm and need-lessly drenching the interior of his house, a valentine card implying that policemen are grafters—he mistakenly jumps to the conclusion that Hamilton is behind them. He thus retaliates with even cruder practical jokes of his own: he has Hamilton arrested on a bogus charge, he sneaks over and lets the air out of Hamilton's automobile tires, and he retaliates with an ugly valentine card. The person really at the bottom of the affair is Gross's other nearby neighbor Martin, a sadistic practical joker who foreshadows Jim Kendall of "Haircut." The "uncivil" neighborhood war ends when Hamilton exposes Martin as the author of the jokes and diverts Gross's anger to the proper target.

The four stories collected in *Own Your Own Home* end with Gross and Hamilton at last on friendly terms with each other; but the three uncollected stories show that the Grosses never gain the social acceptance they so desperately crave. Successively, these stories deal with Gross's attempt to play the stock market, which ends in the loss of his money; his purchase of an automobile, which is stolen before he insures it, but not before he has gone further into debt to build a garage; and his joining the country club and taking up golf, only to resign from the club and vow to quit golf, though his police chief talks him into retaining his clubs so that the two can play together on the municipal links. This last story "Fore!" ranks with the title story "Own Your Own Home" and another entitled "Uncivil War," where Gross's war with Hamilton reaches its peak, as among the best of the series, though no considerable differences in quality exist among the stories as a whole.

The Gross stories again display the inseparable blend of humor and satire which characterizes the busher stories, a blend also typical of other Lardner stories, though the humor of some of those of his major period was so corroded by satire as to be practically nonexistent. The tone of the Gross stories, however, is nearly as dispassionate as that of the busher stories, despite the fact that the reader is sometimes compelled to view Gross as a loathsome slob. The valentine card which Gross spitefully sends his neighbor Hamilton has on it a picture of a fat pig and these verses:

> They ought to keep you in a pen
> Not let you out with other men
> Your not a man but just a big
> Dissgusting stupid greasy pig (98).

The pig metaphor fits Gross himself and is the central image of his character. The fact that Lardner severly blasted policemen in an article he later wrote for *The New Yorker* ("Jersey City Gendarmerie, Je T'Aime") makes it difficult to believe that this portrait of a dumb cop is wholly free from malice. Still, the feeling of contempt aroused in the reader by Gross's boorishness is counterbalanced by a degree of sympathy aroused by the underdog role he plays.

Despite the exaggeration in his portrait of Gross, Lardner nevertheless stops short of caricature. For Gross is a real person who is engaged, however incompetently and crudely, in a real and common American struggle—the effort to rise in the world and to gain for himself and family the material and social benefits which those above him enjoy. Gross's way of fulfilling his aspirations follows the typical American pattern: he builds a new house in a nice neighborhood, he purchases a new car, he buys his wife a piano which she cannot play, he joins the country club and takes up golf. For this reason both Gross and his difficulties have a firm basis in common reality. As one illustration, the troubles he has in building a house are precisely those which the average one-time house builder may actually encounter: he suffers difficulty in obtaining his loan, he and his "archateck" fall out, the contractor walks off the job, and unanticipated extra costs arise to wreck his building budget. The same air of real-life actuality characterizes the other stories; and, though Gross may be a composite character in exhibiting a more excessive aggregation of bad traits than his average real-life counterpart would, his intentions and aims are typically American ones, not simply of Lardner's day, but of our own.

II *Gullible's Travels, Etc.*

A semiliterate roughneck, insensitive to such refinements of civilization as opera and literature, Gullible, the main character of *Gullible's Travels,* bears a kinship to Keefe and Gross. But he is more intelligent and far wiser in the ways of the world than either of them; he is as sardonically amused by his and his wife's follies as he is by those of other people. Narrating his stories orally instead of through letters, he speaks the counterpart of the vernacular idiom that Keefe and Gross write, but he has such a facile command of language that he can usually top his opponent with quick-witted, hardboiled repartee, whereas Keefe and Gross were able only to threaten an opponent with a poke in the jaw. Thus, though Gullible is not as wise as the main character of *The Big Town* and makes errors nearly as ridiculous as those Gross makes, he views the world and his fellow man with a cocksure, knowing eye, sharing Gross's certainty that he is "just as good . . . and a whole lot better" than other people.

Gullible is like Gross too in wanting to advance socially, to become acquainted with members of the "high polloi." His and his wife's efforts to achieve this aim are less crude than those of the Grosses but equally as futile. As big-city apartment dwellers, living on the modest weekly salary which Gullible earns as an office worker, the Gullibles are anonymous members of the great American masses, lacking the advantage of both wealth and education to further their social ambitions. Still, after attending the opera several times and mingling with the socially "E-light," they get "hit" by the "society bacillus" and stop playing cards with their beer-drinking friends, attending picture shows, and going to dance at "Ben's Place." Having thus reached the stage "where our friends wasn't good enough for us no more" (80), they begin dressing up and dining one a week at a big downtown restaurant patronized by the socially prominent. Finally, acting on the absurd notion that proximity to the socially elite will result in acquaintanceships with them, they take an expensive mid-winter trip to Palm Beach, stop at the most fashionable hotel, and, dressed in special resort finery bought for the occasion, they dine, dance, and sit on the beach. But after two weeks, the only contact they have made with high society is Mrs. Gullible's being mistaken for a chambermaid by the wealthy Mrs. Potter of Chicago. Coming to their senses, they return to Chicago, eager to resume relationships with their old friends. Nevertheless, when asked to join the exclusive "San Susie" bridge-playing club, they make a second attempt to become acquainted with people of a higher social and economic rank than theirs; but this one also ends in failure. Though Gullible's sense of humor prevents his being as upset as his wife by these failures, he nevertheless confesses that he enjoyed "wearin' the soup and fish and minglin' amongst the high polloi and pretendin' we really was somebody" (80).

Lardner, however, involves the Gullibles in other activities besides social climbing. Two of the stories deal with the efforts of Gullible's sister-in-law Bess to catch a husband, a theme Lardner also used later in *The Big Town*. Described by Gullible as a person "you couldn't look at without a relapse" (167), Bess strikes up a friendship with a penniless loafer named Bishop; and when marriage appears to be in the offing, Gullible becomes alarmed, foreseeing that support of the couple will devolve on him. Acting on the sardonic thesis that two such people as Bess and Bishop will bore each other to distraction if left solely in each other's company for a time, he takes the couple on a trip and convinces his wife that they should leave the two "love birds" to themselves. After two days, disgusted with each other's self-conceit and dullness, Bess and Bishop part in anger; and when Gullible's "Missus" later wonders "what could of happened" between the two, Gullible tells her: "I know what happened. . . . They got acquainted" (208).

The central situations of the stories, such as the love affair of the fatuous Bess and Bishop, the trip to Palm Beach, and the efforts of the Gullibles to qualify for membership in the "San Susie" bridge club, serve as the major focal points for the satire in *Gullible's Travels*. The leisured development of these situations, however, allowed Lardner ample opportunity to intro-duce many incidental characters and thus to place his main characters in the larger setting of middle-class American life.

Often the reader gets a brief but telling glimpse of these incidental characters—a fat citizen on a train, for example, giving Gullible the low-down on President Wilson's foreign policy: "He either ought to of went stronger or not so strong" (99); or a couple in a hotel dining room with the domineering wife countermanding every order her husband gives the waiter. But at other times, Lardner presents these incidental characters in a mass, as when he describes through Gullible the motley weekend crowd on the Chicago—St. Joe steamer: identical looking cube-shaped, apple-eating mothers, holding identical-looking, squalling babies in their arms; young couples reeling on the dance floor; a drunk standing at the bar "all lit up like the municipal pier" and monotonously repeating the phrase "Too rough! Too rough!" (192-93), a phrase which epitomizes the whole scene.

Regardless of whether they are lower-class people drinking and dancing their way through a weekend boat trip, tourists flocking to resort hotels to sit on the beach and stare at their own kind, or financially well-heeled bridge-players whose sleek dress clothes fail to provide them with the social veneer needed to check the eruption of their nasty tempers, Gullible views the antics of his fellow Americans with ironic amusement. Even though he thus becomes an in-character mouthpiece for Lardner, Gullible is not presented as a detached observer of life, disassociated from the people he criticizes, but as an active participant in that life, a representative member of hoi polloi. Indeed, Lardner clearly presents Gullible as a kind of common denominator of the flatness, barrenness, and vulgarity of middle-class American life, not so crude as the drunk in the barroom—or so vile-tempered as Gullible's "elite" bridge hostess, but a nameless, average, white-collar citizen.

Gullible has self-awareness enough to realize who he is and what he is, but he also has an easy self-assurance, and it is this trait which obscures his self-preception and makes him gullible. Knowing practically nothing about bridge-playing, he allows his wife, also a novice player, to lead him into a game with experts, his self-assurance deluding him into thinking that somehow he and the "missus" will come through the affair with honor and fine new friends. Fully realizing that he and his wife possess none of the real prerequisites needed for achieving social prominence, he is prompted to make the effort against nearly impossible odds, not only playing the long-shot chance in the typical American manner, but even confessing that he enjoyed the attempt. As ignorant of opera as his wife, Gullible gains possession of a libretto and has the brash confidence to retell the story of the opera in his own words for the edification of his wife: "*Carmen* ain't no regular musical show were a couple o' Yids comes out and pulls a few lines o' dialogue and then a girl and a he-flirt sings a song that ain't got nothin' to do with it. *Carmen's* a regular play, only instead o' them sayin' the lines, they sing them, and in for'n languages so's the actors can pick up some loose change offen the sale o' the liberettos" (14).

In his essay, "Ring Lardner and the Triangle of Hate," Clifton Fadiman cites the foregoing passage as an illustration of a speech which "punctures opera and American popular entertainment at the same time that it casually rips the cover off the cheap mind of the speaker."[1] At every turn, Lardner does expose the cheapness and mediocrity of Gullible's mind; and since Gullible represents the common American citizen Lardner thus makes through him a satiric commentary on a large segment of the American populace. But there is no rancor in this satire. Granted that the view of American society implied in *Gullible's Travels* is disquieting—a social structure made up of vast numbers of gullibles must inevitably be regarded as a flimsy one—there are nevertheless no implications that the country has gone, or will go, "to the dogs" because it is populated by gullibles. As was his usual habit, Lardner was satisfied to present the case in specific and concrete detail and to let the reader draw such conclusions as he might, or—failing to perceive that the shoe fits—to treat the work as humor and nonsense.

III *The Big Town*

Although it deals with a theme and a set of characters by now a little shopworn, *The Big Town* is one of the most interesting works of fiction Lardner produced because it represents his literary talent near its peak and it presents a revelatory picture of American society in the immediate postwar years of 1920 and 1921. The theme is stated in the subtitle the work carries: "How I and the Mrs. Go to New York to see Life and Get Katie A Husband." Katie, the husband-seeker, "twenty years old and pretty and full of peace and good will towards men" (195), is the sister of the narrator's wife, Ella. The narrator himself is a South Bend, Indiana, cigar salesman named Finch, who is more quick-witted in his repartee and more caustic in his criticism of other people than Gullible. The husband-hunting trip is made possible by the fortune left to Ella and Katie by their dead stepfather, a war-profiteer from Niles, Michigan. After several futile efforts to turn up an eligible suitor for Katie in South Bend, Ella persuades the narrator to take her and Katie to New York, "where they's life and fun; where we can meet real live people" (13).

Though Katie has apparently made an early conquest when she meets a slick-tongued Wall Street broker on the train, it develops later in New York that the broker is himself intent on making a conquest, not of Katie, but of Ella; and the result is that Finch goes to the broker's Wall Street office and beats him up. Undaunted by the outcome of this affair, Katie keeps trying: she attracts a wealthy bachelor but, finding him as old as "Methuselah," she begins an affair with his chauffeur, and then breaks it off when she discovers that the chauffeur is married. She thinks the young airplane inventor whom she next meets is the right man until he is killed in a plane crash. She perversely resists the marriage proposal of Daley, a wealthy owner of racing horses, preferring the attentions of Mercer, the tough little jockey who rides Daley's horses; but she drops Mercer after she learns that he once served a jail sentence. In the end, attracted by the glamor of Broadway show business and deluded by the false notion that a professional comedian will keep her amused, she marries Ralston, a comedian who plays bit parts in the Ziegfeld Follies and is "terribly funny when he gets just the right number of drinks" (198). With well-justified qualms about a marriage based more on Katie's attraction to the stage and Ralston's attraction to her money than on mutual affection, the narrator and his wife return to South Bend with a renewed appreciation of the virtues of a town smaller than New York.

Toward the end of the trio's adventures in New York, the narrator confesses that he has gotten past minding the ordeal of struggling into his dress clothes because "They was one advantage in dolling up every time you went anywheres. It meant an hour when they was no chance to do something even sillier" (201). This remark keynotes the viewpoint Lardner expressed through his characters in *The Big Town*: that the behavior of human beings—at least the American types presented in this book—though less silly on some occasions than on others, is nevertheless characteristically and typically silly. With the exception of Finch, the ironic narrator, who continually exerts himself to prevent the two women from doing foolish things, but who yet allows himself to become a working partner in their folly, the characters of *The Big Town* appear to be engaged in a contest to outdo each other in the foolishness of their behavior, and all win awards. Katie, of course, is a leading contender: nearly the only good thing that can be said for her is that she is sexually moral; beyond that, she has no judgment, no sense of values, no taste, no depth of character. She can engage her affections easily, but she disengages them just as easily. After the death of one suitor in the crash of the airplane he has invented, for example, the narrator remarks to Ella that they would probably be living "in a vale of tears for the next several days," but Ella promptly reassures him to the contrary: "No," said Ella. "Sis is taking it pretty calm. She's sensible. She says if that could of happened, why the invention couldn't of been no good after all. And the Williamses probably wouldn't of give him a plugged dime for it" (134).

In general, the whole battery of characters is a vain and foolish lot, devoid alike of principles and taste—the brash young broker who mistakenly thinks Ella will be an easy pick-up, the idle-brained, wealthy old bachelor who yearns for a youthful mate and makes a hobby of collecting dressing gowns and bathrobes, the crooked jockey Mercer who throws the race, the vain stupid Ralston who pretends that he freely gives his gag-lines to other comedians but who in reality takes theirs for his own use. Not even the narrator is above compromising his principles. Learning that the jockey Mercer plans to pull back Daley's prize horse to let a second-rater win, Finch withholds the information from Daley and wins a pile of money by betting on the second-rater, while the bewildered Daley loses fifteen thousand dollars backing his horse in the same race. Though Finch's conscience pricks him a little—"I don't know if you'll think I done right or not" (186)—he quickly rationalizes his action on the grounds that Daley has said ugly things about him and Ella and that the jockey would have inflicted bodily injuries on him had he exposed the crooked deal.

Nearly everything from horse-racing to war-profiteering, from snobbish bridge-players to young shimmy dancers, from over-stuffed idle rich people to vain show people, comes under the lash of Lardner's satire in *The Big Town*. Here, for example, is the picture he gives through his ironic narrator of the inhabitants of a Long Island family-type hotel, where "a few of the couples that can't afford dogs has got children, and you are always tripping over one or the other":

> The men get up about eight o'clock and go down to New York to Business. They don't never go to work. About nine the women begins limping downstairs and either goes to call on their dogs or take them for a walk in the front yard. This is a great big yard with a whole lot of benches strewed round it, but you can't set on them in the daytime because the women or the nurses uses them for a place to read to the dogs or kids, and in the evenings you would have to share them with the waitresses, which you have already had enough of them during the day.
>
> When the women has prepared themselves for the long day's grind with a four-course breakfast, they set round on the front porch and discuss the big questions of the hour, like for instance the last trunk murder or whether an Airedale is more loving than a Golden Bantam. Once in a wile one of them cracks that it looks like they was bound to be a panic pretty soon and a big drop in prices, and so forth. This shows they're broad-minded and are giving a good deal of thought to up-to-date topics. Every so often one of them'll say: "The present situation can't keep up." The hell it can't! (96-97).

Even without Elder's assurance that Lardner had moved his family to a Long Island family-type hotel sometime before writing the above passage, one might have surmised that it was based on direct observation. So too the description below of people attending the horse races on a Saturday afternoon:

> Lots of them was gals that you'd have to have a pick to break through to their regular face. Since they had their last divorce, about the only excitement they could enjoy was playing a long shot. Which reminds me that they's an old saying that nobody loves a fat man, but you go out to a race track or down to Atlantic City or any place where the former wifes hangs out and if you'll notice the birds with them, the gents that broke up their home, you'll find out that the most of them is guys with chins that runs into five or six figures and once round their waist is a sleeper jump. (151-52).

With their own pockets full of the money Ella and Katie's step-father made selling overpriced leather to the government during the war, the Finches are *nouveau riche* idlers themselves, throwing money away on amusements, ritzy apartments, and fancy clothiers. They are thus fully as typical of the postwar society of the early 1920's which Lardner is satirizing in *The Big Town* as are the overstuffed, dog-loving, bridge-playing residents of the family hotel or the corpulent men and their heavily made-up "Janes" at the race track. The sardonic comment Lardner puts in the mouth of an automobile salesman neatly summarizes the money-mad, status-seeking activity of the people of that period—and perhaps of this one. The Finches have gone to the salesman intending to purchase an automobile they do not need, but they find the automobile both overpriced and unavailable. The salesman tells Finch, "Listen . . . I'll be frank with you. We got the New York agency for this car and was glad to get it because it sells for four thousand and anything that sells that high, why the people will eat up, even if it's a pearl-handle ketchup bottle. If we ever do happen to get a consignment of these cars, they'll sell like oil stock" (66).

As these passages amply testify, by the time Lardner came to write *The Big Town*—it should be remembered that its five chapters were published at widely spaced intervals between March, 1920 and May, 1921—he was already showing signs of the thorough disenchantment with the American scene which characterizes his work from around 1923 on. The satire of *The Big Town* has a deadlier sting and is applied to a wider segment of American life than that of any of the works so far discussed. Yet, regardless of the harshness of Lardner's indictment of such individuals as the vain Ralston, the snobbish Lady Perkins, and the rich Mrs. Snell or of such entire groups of people as overfed idlers dwelling in suburban hotels, morally bankrupt race-track fans, and of masses of people recklessly throwing away money on overpriced luxuries, Lardner still permits the reader to view the main characters sympathetically. With the exception of the single breach of ethical principles involved in the crooked horse race and perhaps of the fact that he sees no reason why he should not live on his wife's money since he is legally married to her, the narrator is presented as a basically decent human being, seeing through the shallow pretensions and hyprocrisies of his fellow man and quick to defend the family honor when a man makes a pass at his wife. Ella is a fitting mate for him, able to give nearly as good as she receives in the exchange of ironic remarks, and even the silly Katie is not wholly ridiculed. Moreover, some of the minor characters are presented as respectable human beings—for example, the unfortunate young aviator and Daley the race-horse owner—and sometimes even those who are ridiculed are displayed in a warmly human light, as when Trumbull, the wealthy old bachelor, is shown kneeling in his dress clothes on the expensive, imported rug in his gaudy apartment to roll dice with the narrator and implore "Eighter from Decatur" to show. From the busher stories on, Lardner had been "writing about humanity at large," as Gilbert Seldes has remarked, but ". . . in *The Big Town*, the field of reference is wider; the appreciation of human character is more generous; the creation of a whole fraction of society is more powerfully and completely done."[2]

IV *Style and Technique*

In *Own Your Own Home*, Lardner used the epistolary technique he had perfected in *You Know Me Al* and continued to use in subsequent groups of busher stories—that of having an illiterate main character, totally unconscious of how vividly his language deformities reflect the crudities and inadequacies of his mental processes, narrate the stories through the letters he writes. But in *Gullible's Travels* and *The Big Town*, Lardner abandoned the letter-writer-narrator for a first-person oral narrator who speaks instead of writes the vernacular idiom; the result is that these two works are similiar to each other in style though different stylistically from *Own Your Own Home*.

The style of *Own Your Own Home* is characterized by language illiteracies more excessive than those of the busher stories, for though Jack Keefe committed every language atrocity imaginable, Fred Gross commits the same atrocities on a grander and more consistent scale. Jack, for example, did manage to spell a substantial number of his words correctly, but there are few that Gross can spell correctly, and his misspellings result in malapropisms which frequently have a suggestive overtone similar to those of Danny Warner in *Lose with a Smile*. In some cases the misspelled word creates a comic effect but at the same time conveys the right idea: Gross spells "whooping" in whooping cough as "whopping" and the cough is after all a whopping one. More typically, however, the misspelling produces an idea which is the opposite of the one intended: when the basic American doctrine that "all men are created free" passes under Gross's stubby pen it is transformed into another doctrine— "all men are crated free." Moreover, while Keefe's sentences are frequently long and involved, they are not so long—or so tortuously involved—as Gross's are. Here is a fair sample:

> And Im going to cut out the booze all together and of coarse you know I aint the kind that guzzles it down like I was scarred they was going to quit selling it though I can hold a bbl. of it and not never show no affect but I dont never take more than say 5 or 6 drinks a day and mostly beer at that but it runs in to money because you dont feel like buying for yourself and none of your friends and they aint a bar where I go in to that they aint 1 or 2 of my freinds in there and I got as many freinds is the next man but they aint none of them that sores there throte up saying No thanks or Have another or stranes there biceps halling out there money to buy back.[3]

To relieve the slow movement of long sentences of this type, however, Lardner also made his character sometimes use short sentences or speed up the movement of long ones by repeating short, parallel clauses, as in this passage in which Gross repeats a lesson he has learned from a pro about his poor golfing form: "So I says Well whats the matter with me. So he says Nothing only you went back too fast and you took your left ft. off of the ground, and you took your eyes off of the ball and you moved your head and you stood too far away from the ball and you dident take no aim at where you was shooting at and you tried to kill it and you pulled away from it like it was a snake or something."[4] Besides giving variety to the style, the staccato rhythm of the above sentence reflects the golf pro's caustic mood, but the rhythmical beat of the sentences, regardless of whether they are long or short ones, typically is appropriate to the mood of the character. For example, in a towering rage, Gross bawls out a garage mechanic: "You cheap stiff I says. Your a wise guy I says. And theys another thing you ought to guess without nobody telling you and thats what to use soap for. But if you ever seen a cake of soap I says you must of thought it was cheese and ett it. You big cheese I told him."[5]

Despite the effectiveness of variations in rhythm and sentence patterns, the prose of the Gross stories lacks the color, verve, and force of that of the busher stories. In part, the difference may be that Lardner was less certain about how a dumb policeman would express himself in writing than he was about how a dumb baseball player would. It is true nevertheless that Gross's language atrocities reflect the atrocity of his mind and that his hopeless ensnarlment in the web of his sentence structure is the counterpart of his hopeless ensnarlment in the web of life. But the excessive illiteracy becomes tiresome, and perhaps it is fortunate that Lardner abandoned his stupid cop after using him in seven stories.

Perhaps it was fortunate too that Lardner chose to write at least two of his nine groups of connected short stories from the point of view of an oral rather than an epistolary narrator. For regardless of the fact that Lardner's imitation of spoken vernacular American depended for its authenticity on language distortions nearly as much as his imitation of its written form, *Gullible's Travels* and *The Big Town* nevertheless afford a welcome relief from the epistolary style. The grammatical irregularities involved in the style of these two works are so much a part of the vernacular idiom the characters use and so fully absorbed into the easy, rhythmical flow of their speech that they are far less noticeable than those of his epistolary style; and the sentences are shorter, with a faster tempo. Most obviously, however, the use of an oral narrator allowed Lardner to reduce drastically the frequency of spelling errors, and the misspellings that do occur—such typical ones, for example, as *idear, offen, oncet, acrost, wile, ast*—are used as much for the purpose of reproducing the sound of the characters' speech as for displaying their illiteracy. For the same reason, Gullible is made to use such contractions as *li'ble, op'ra, s'pose, clo'es, to'rds* and to drop the final *g* from most words ending in *-ing*, though not from all. For Lardner's accurate ear had detected that in "common American" the *g* is dropped from *somethin'* and *nothin'* but not from *anything* and *everything*. "There appears to be somethin' about the *y* near the middle of both these words," he said, "that impels us to acknowledge the *g* on the end of them."[6]

But interestingly enough, in *The Big Town* Lardner made his narrator retain the final *g*'s and use fewer contractions; it would be difficult to say whether these changes reflect subtle differences

Lardner had observed in the speech habits of Indiana Hoosiers and Chicago office workers or merely represent a minor refinement of his style. But whatever the case, the vernacular style of *Gullible's Travels* and *The Big Town* gains its accuracy from Lardner's use of grammatical irregularities more basic than contractions and dropped *g*'s. Both Gullible and Finch misuse verb forms, tenses, and pronouns; and while their shorter, spoken sentences enable them to avoid the long, involved structure typical of those Gross used in his letters, they still occasionally tie their sentences into nearly inconceivable grammatical knots. There is little wrong with the following sentence, where Finch is describing the conveniences available at his hotel, except the phrase at the end of it—but what a twist that is! "They even got a barber and a valet, but you can't get a shave wile he's pressing your clothes, so it's pretty near impossible for a man to look their best at the same time" (*The Big Town*, 99). And again this sentence, used by Finch's wife to point out to him the supposed advantages of leasing an expensive apartment, is quite similar to one Jack Keefe would use: "It won't only be for about a year and it's in the nicest kind of a neighborhood and we can't meet nothing only the best kind of people" (*The Big Town*, 56).

Despite the appearance of such deformities as those in the sentences above, however, the style of *Gullible's Travels* and *The Big Town* illustrates the sure knowledge Lardner had that "as a rule, our language is not looking for trouble."[7] The language errors Gullible, Finch, and the other characters in *Gullible's Travels* and *The Big Town* make are those typical of common American speech—*I seen, we was, would of, ain't got* and so on. Like the millions of Americans they represent, the characters are unaware of grammatical subtleties; and, in grabbing hold of the language and forcing it to convey their thoughts with a minimum of ease, they have no "idear" that they make mistakes. Their barbarisms nevertheless fail to blunt the cutting edge of the living speech they use. In the following passage, for example, Finch has already squelched Griffin, the city slicker, once but has to squelch him again:

> "You're a smart Aleck," he said. "But speaking about war, where was you?"
> "In the shipyards at South Bend painting a duck boat," I says. "And where was you?"

"I'd of been in there in a few more weeks," he says. "They wasn't no slackers in the Big Town."

"No," said I, "and America will never forget New York for coming in on our side" (*The Big Town*, 26).

Finally, one notes the authentic ring of dialogue in the following passage, in which the Finches and Katie are exchanging viewpoints on Ralston, the Follies comedian:

"Well," said Ella, "how do you like him?"

"I think he's wonderful!" says Katie. "I didn't have no idear he was so deep, wanting to play Hamlet."

"Pretty near all comedians has got that bug," I says.

"Maybe he's different when you know him better," said Ella.

"I don't want him to be different," says Kate.

"But he was so serious," said the Mrs. "He didn't say nothing funny."

"Sure he did," I says. "Didn't he say artists hate to talk about themselfs?"

Pretty soon the waiter come in with our lunch. He ast us if the other gentleman was coming back.

"No," said Ella. "He's through."

"He forgot his check," says the dish smasher.

"Oh, never mind!" says Ella. "We'll take care of that."

"Well," I says, "I guess the bird was telling the truth when he said he didn't need no money" (*The Big Town*, 210-11).

This passage serves to remind one that Lardner used the vernacular idiom, not as an end itself, but as a means of revealing the qualities of his characters' minds, of making them project themselves to the reader as real people, true to their type. The rounded-off simplicity of Katie's "I didn't have no idear he was so deep, wanting to play Hamlet" and Ella's "maybe he's different when you get to know him" expose the uncomplicated directness and simplicity of their mental processes, as Finch's "dish smasher" phrase keeps him typed in his "wise guy" role. Lardner ". . . used conversation as a dramatist uses it, to let you into the secrets of the heart," Gilbert Seldes said, and noted further: "You never say, 'people don't talk that way' when you read Lardner; people do talk that way because people *are* that way."[8]

Turning from style to other phases of the technique of *Own Your Own Home*, *Gullible's Travels*, and *The Big Town*, we find that the two first works follow an organizational scheme quite similar to that of the busher stories. That is, in each story a single major episode in the lives of the characters is developed which may give rise to the one developed in the next story or may have no direct bearing on it. If anything, the stories are more self-contained than the busher stories; and while there are advantages in reading them in chronological order, they can be understood when read in any order—particularly the *Gullible* group and the last three stories in the *Own Your Own Home* series.

The same thing, however, cannot be said of *The Big Town* group. The five chapters or "stories" of that work develop progressively a single major theme which is brought to a climax in the action and resolved: the Finches go to New York to see life and find Katie a husband; on the fifth attempt Katie lands a husband, and the Finches return gratefully to South Bend. Consequently, even though each chapter centers on a separate adventure the trio has on the life-seeing, husband-hunting expedition, the five chapters are not easily detachable separate units but interdependent parts of a larger work, to be understood properly only when read in sequential order, as are the chapters of a novel. For this reason, the structure of *The Big Town* so closely resembles that of a novel that it seems less arbitrary to describe the work as a novel than as a collection of short stories. Still, the work is loosely and episodically organized: Lardner could have developed his theme in more steps or perhaps even in fewer without materially altering the result. Thus, if it is inaccurate to define *The Big Town* as a collection of short stories, the work can be defined as a novel only by using that term broadly.

In connection with the mooted question of what fictional category *The Big Town* most properly fits, it is significant to note that Lardner himself insisted that novels lay beyond the scope of his talent. In 1925, for instance, on the basis of interviews with Lardner, Grant Overton reported that "he thinks he could never write a novel";[9] and in a piece he wrote for *The New Yorker* in 1930, Lardner mentioned that he had turned down a request from "the Scribner boys" for "a full-length novel or book on one subject . . . on the ground that I couldn't think of a subject I could stretch into a novel or book."[10] Even though it is evident from *The Big Town* and perhaps also from

The Busher Re-enlists and *Lose with a Smile* that the position Lardner took on novel-writing was another example of his self-deprecation, it is also true that from the beginning he wrote his fiction for the popular magazine market and that the short-story form suited his purposes more fully than the novel form could. Once having formed the habit of writing stories designed to appear by installments in a loosely connected series dealing with common characters, or as separate stories dealing with entirely different characters, he perhaps became convinced that he could write fiction in no other mode.

Whatever may be the full explanation of Lardner's viewpoint regarding his inability to write novels, it is clear that he found the transition from writing sequence groups to writing separate short stories an easy one to make. Though he had steadily produced separate stories from 1914 to 1921, he devoted his main efforts in this period to the sequence groups; but with the single exception of *Lose with a Smile,* he wrote no more such groups after *The Big Town,* thereafter devoting his major efforts to separate short stories.

In style and technique, as well as in their characters and subject matter, *Own Your Own Home, Gullible's Travels,* and *The Big Town* are as distinctly in the native American tradition as are the busher stories. In these three works Lardner depicted three new major characters; and even though there are resemblances among them, the three types, together with the numerous new minor characters he introduced, go far toward suggesting the tone and temper of the whole fabric of middle-class American life. Moreover, while Lardner gave a less satisfying demonstration of his ability to handle the epistolary form of the vernacular idiom in *Own Your Own Home* than he had given in the Keefe stories, he displayed in *Gullible's Travels* and *The Big Town* a perfect mastery of the oral form of the idiom. In vivacity, the style of *The Big Town* is not excelled by that of any other work he produced. For this reason, as well as for its other qualities, *The Big Town* holds a position among the nine groups of sequence stories at least as important as that held by *You Know Me Al.*

CHAPTER 4

The Turning Point:
How to Write Short Stories

DURING the highly productive first decade of his career, from 1914 to 1924, Lardner published not only the eight groups of sequence stories discussed in the two preceding chapters but also twenty-eight individual stories not belonging to a connected group. He chose to reprint only ten of the twenty-eight in *How to Write Short Stories,* his first of three collections of separate stories. The volume marked a turning point in his career, for it placed a representative sampling of the best fiction he had thus far produced in the hands of literary critics who quickly perceived that his was the work of an accomplished and serious literary artist.

In June, 1924, shortly after the appearance of *How to Write Short Stories,* Maxwell Perkins, the Scribner editor who handled the publishing arrangements, called Lardner's attention to an article in *Printers' Ink* which was "highly complimentary to the device of the title and preface . . . as being a new way of putting out a product so as to distinguish it."[1] To the contrary, these features—not only the title and the burlesque preface but also the zany notes introducing each story—are inappropriate and detract from rather than enhance the volume.

The preface purports to give "boys and gals who wants to take up writing as their life work . . . a few hints in regards to the technic of the short story, how to go about planning it and writing it, when and where to plant the love interest and climax, and finally how to market the finished product without leaving no bad taste in the mouth" (p. vi).[2] Continuing in this vein, the preface is an obvious take-off on the fiction handbook which had been called into existence in the late 1890's by the introduction of short-story writing courses into college and correspondence school curricula.

Based chiefly on the dogmatic tenets of Brander Matthews' "The Philosophy of the Short-story" (1885), these handbooks prescribed rules for the guidance of the aspiring author and promised him success if he followed them. The high prices that mass-circulation magazines began paying for stories in the early decades of the twentieth century—Lardner was once offered $3,000 each for his next six stories or $3,500 each for his next twelve (See Elder, p. 219)—drew vast numbers of literary hopefuls to story writing and created such a demand for "practical treatises" on the subject that by 1920 "the literature of the grim mechanics of short-story writing" threatened to become as "voluminous as the short stories themselves."[3] Thus, just as the "Little Sunbeams of Success" parodies Lardner wrote for the *Cosmopolitan* in 1922 derided the American belief in quick and easy success in the business world, so the preface to *How to Write Short Stories* derided the idea promoted by the handbooks that success in the "writing game" was easily attainable: "You can't find no school in operation up to date . . . which can make a great author out of a born druggist" (p. vi).

But granting that the spoofing preface of the volume can be applauded for ridiculing the notion of easy success in writing, both it and the introductory notes are out of tune with the serious import of the stories in the volume. To introduce "The Golden Honeymoon" as an example of "a story with 'sex appeal'" or "My Roomy" as a "delightful tale of life in the Kiwanis Club" appears rather gauche; and Lardner's description of "Champion" as a "mystery" story—the mystery being "how it came to get printed"—is self-debasing rather than humorous. Clearly, the preface and notes provide another illustration of Lardner's refusal to regard his work seriously or to admit publicly that he was a literary artist. Fitzgerald noted that the stories in *How to Write Short Stories* had to be photographed from back numbers of magazines in which they had appeared: "My God! he had not even saved them";[4] this fact itself reflects Lardner's astonishing indifference to his work. In his 1924 review of *How to Write Short Stories*, Edmund Wilson said that Lardner "seems committed to popular journalism" and "does not even care to admit that he has tried to do work on a higher level— hence the clownish presentation of these stories."[5] As Wilson observed, the volume should have been called *The Champion and Other Stories.*

The clowning presentation of *How to Write Short Stories* fails, however, to obscure the intrinsic merit of the stories in the volume. Even though four of the ten are of only average quality, three—"Champion," "Some Like Them Cold," and "The Golden Honeymoon"—are among the best Lardner ever wrote. Three others—"My Roomy," "A Caddy's Diary," and "Alibi Ike"— are only slightly less noteworthy. Despite the fact that six of the stories deal with the world of professional sports, that nine are told in the first person either by oral or epistolary narrators, and that a number have similar structural patterns, the ten stories as a group are varied in theme and in character. None, of course, so well illustrates this variety or so fully shows Lardner in his best vein as the three best ones do.

I   *The Prizefighter Debunked*

"Champion," the first of the three in order of appearance, is distinguished both by the excellence of its technique and by its presentation of the most vicious character found in the entire compass of Lardner's fiction—Midge Kelly a prizefighter. Lacking even the faintest shred of human decency, Kelly is a merciless bully who brutally punches his way through the world, landing knockout blows on relatives and friends as well as on foes in the boxing ring. He "scored his first knockout when he was seventeen. The knockee was his brother Connie, three years his junior and a cripple" (145). His own mother becomes his second victim, for, when she remonstrates with him about his attack on Connie, he knocks her to the floor and leaves home for good. Going to Milwaukee, he wins a fight, accepts a bribe to throw another, and seduces the sister of a friend who has been buying his food and drinks. Forced to marry the girl, he delivers a crushing blow to "the bride's pale face" on the wedding night and goes to Boston. Destitute in a bar he encounters Tommy Haley, who stakes him to a new start and becomes his manager. Under Haley's wise management he becomes a champion, but he dumps Haley with the threat of physical violence at the suggestion of his new girl friend Grace, whom he also gets rid of when his roving eye settles on the handsome wife of his new manager, Harris. Taking Harris' wife and firing Harris from the manager's job, Kelly goes to New York, where he is soon booked for a big fight under the management of Wallie Adams.

In the concluding scene, which occurs on the eve of this fight, a reporter comes to Kelly's training quarters to seek information needed for the feature article his paper has assigned him to write on Kelly. Unable to see Kelly, the reporter gets the "facts" he uses in his story from manager Wallie:

> "Just a kid; that's all he is; a regular boy. Get what I mean? Don't know the meanin' o' bad habits. Never tasted liquor in his life and would prob'bly get sick if he smelled it. Clean livin' put him up where he's at. Get what I mean? And modest and unassumin' as a school girl. He's so quiet you wouldn't never know he was round. And he'd go to jail before he'd talk about himself.
>
> "No job at all to get him in shape, 'cause he's always that way. The only trouble we have with him is gettin' him to light into these poor bums they match him up with. He's scared he'll hurt somebody. Get what I mean?" (175).

The manager goes on at length, presenting Kelly as the direct opposite of the vicious character that he actually is; but Lardner ends the story with a still further twist of irony. If the reporter had had access to the real facts of Kelly's life and had based his story on them instead of the manager's falsehoods, the sporting editor would not have printed it. " 'Suppose you can prove it,' that gentleman would have said, 'It wouldn't get us anything but abuse to print it. The people don't want him knocked. He's champion' " (178).

Thus, in "The Champion" Lardner fires a double-barreled satiric charge, first at the depraved brutality of prize fighting which rewards the vicious qualities Midge Kelly possessed, and second at the "anile idolatory" of athletes by the public which converts a character as despicable as Midge Kelly into a paragon of virtue. Despite the indignant or even furious attitude which evidently underlies the story, Lardner wrote it in a quiet, matter-of-fact tone, the very calmness of which enhances the powerful effect of the story and conforms to the objective method Lardner invariably used. Written in the third person with few authorial intrusions, the story unfolds through approximately a dozen key scenes—Midge shown knocking out his brother, agreeing to "lay down" in a fight for eighty dollars, scornfully reading letters from his mother and wife asking for money, telling Haley to leave, and so on. Each scene emerges from the one before and leads to the next, the whole sequence culminating in the sardonic irony of the final scene where the reporter interviews Wallie.

Distributing the action of a story over a sequence of numerous small scenes in this manner instead of concentrating it in a few major ones creates two technical problems: first, that of maintaining dramatic intensity in the sequence of scenes and, second, that of handling the transitions between scenes with a minimum of interruption in the flow of the action. The first of these problems Lardner solved by making each scene "a picture taken from a different angle,"[6] so that as the scenes multiply, the tension mounts. He solved the second by the simple device of leaving a break in the text, so that the reader moves immediately from the action of one scene into that of the next. The one major exception is a break near the middle of the story where it was necessary for Lardner to give the reader a flash-back covering a time-gap of almost two years, but he presented it dramatically through the conversation of two minor characters.

In another instance, Lardner restored to the timeworn device of giving exposition through letters which Midge receives in the same mail from his abandoned wife, his mother, and his mistress, Grace. Successively, they reveal (1) that his baby will die unless his impoverished wife receives money to buy better food for it, (2) that his brother Connie has been unable to get out of bed in over three years and that a letter from Midge will be better for Connie "then a barl of medisin," (3) that Grace hopes Midge's opponent in a forthcoming fight won't spoil "my baby's pretty face" and that she needs "a couple hundred" sent to her by wire. Though Midge sends Grace the money requested, he displays his cold-hearted viciousness by tearing up the letters from his wife and his mother. It may have been the extreme contrast presented in this scene between Midge's affluence and the poverty of his family which moved Donald Elder to remark that " 'Champion' . . . is far too melodramatic to be entirely believable" (208). But, even though Lardner plainly stacks the cards against his vicious bully, the scene lays the groundwork for the supreme irony of the concluding one, without which the story would have little meaning. Thus, in its dispassionate presentation of as loathesome a character as can be found in modern fiction, "Champion" is a remarkable exhibition of Lardner's technical skill.

II   *The Battle of the Sexes*

By contrast, "Some Like Them Cold" and "The Golden Honey-moon" present characters far less black-hearted than Midge Kelly, and though Lardner also made them the object of satire, he displayed in neither story the coldly furious attitude exhibited in "Champion." To the contrary, his blend of irony and humor is such as to make the reader aware of the defects the characters have without making him censure them as he must Midge Kelly. Although the fatuous young couple in "Some Like Them Cold" and the empty-headed old couple in "Golden Honeymoon" are rather miserable examples of humanity, they nevertheless are more representative types than Midge Kelly; consequently, they assume a broader significance in Lardner's gallery of characters than he does.

"Some Like Them Cold" is the story of an affair of the heart which develops between Mabelle Gillespie and Charles Lewis when the two meet in a Chicago railroad station as Lewis is departing for New York to seek fame as a song-writer. Narrated through letters the couple exchanges, the story shows Charles at first leading Mabelle on and then Mabelle, now strongly interested, presenting through her letters an image of herself designed to attract Charles to the altar: she is a homebody and a good cook, she does not use make-up because she has a naturally sound complexion, she is a great talker but also likes to read the "highbrow" poetry of Robert W. Service, she has been left money by her father but prefers earning her living to idleness. But as Mabelle warms up, Charles having met new friends in New York, cools off. Finally, he ends the affair by telling Mabelle that he is engaged to marry a girl who, though "a cold fish" and "show crazy," is "some doll," a person with traits and interests the opposite of Mabelle's. But the crowning touch to Mabelle's humiliation is Charles's advice to "never speak to strange men who you don't know nothing about as they may get you wrong and think you are trying to make them. It just happened that I knew better so you was lucky in my case but the luck might not last" (78).

Whether consciously intended or not, the interesting play on opposites—particularly on those of "hot" and "cold"—which runs through the story reinforces the battle of the sexes theme. Further, Lardner's puritanism regarding sexual matters failed to prevent his introducing a covert note of sexualism into the story through Charles's references to sleeping in his underwear and lying in the bath tub and Mabelle's allusions to how frequently and cleanly she bathes herself. Still, by such touches as these Lardner makes the young man and woman round out their own portraits and fully expose the cheapness and vulgarity of their minds. Lardner's epistolary technique was never better demonstrated than in this story.

"The Golden Honeymoon," however, is an equally masterful demonstration of Lardner's use of another narrative method—the oral monologue. The story again presents the battle of the sexes theme, this time through a couple of advanced age. Married fifty years and in their seventies, the narrator and his wife take a midwinter trip to St. Petersburg, Florida, to escape the rigors of the Northern climate. In the manner typical of thousands of such couples who go to St. Petersburg for the same reason, the two old people spend their time watching others play, or playing themselves, such games as checkers, roque, and horseshoes; but, old as they are, they still exhibit both the competitiveness and egotism which nearly all of Lardner's characters possess. The narrator gloats over his ability to defeat in checker games his wife's former suitor, Hartsell; but he peevishly claims that a sore thumb prevents his defeating Hartsell at horseshoe pitching. Mrs. Hartsell and the narrator's wife play a game of roque, but "Mother couldn't hit a flea and they all laughed at her" (135), and Mrs. Hartsell is terribly chagrined when she loses her false teeth on the court. A flare-up of jealousy, provoked by the presence of "Mother's" old suitor, keeps the couple from speaking to each other for two days, but they make up: ". . . I put my arm around her shoulder and she stroked my hand and I guess we got kind of spoony" (140).

Noting that "The Golden Honeymoon" was Lardner's favorite story, Donald Elder calls attention to the fact that it "aroused varying reactions." George Horace Lorimer of the *Saturday Evening Post* irked Lardner when he rejected the story as being "too far from [Lardner's] usual line," but Ray Long of the *Cosmopolitan*, who gladly paid $1,500 for it, regarded it as a fine piece of sympathetic human interest writing, as did Gilbert Seldes, who thought Lardner had treated the old man in the story with "loving kindness."[7] At the other extreme, however, Clifton Fadiman described the story as "one of the most smashing indictments of a 'happy marriage' ever written, composed with a fury so gelid as to hide completely the bitter passion seething beneath every line. Under the level of homey sentiment lies a terrific contempt for this quarrelsome, vain, literal old couple who for fifty years have disliked life and each other without ever having had the courage or the imagination to face the reality of their meanness."[8] William Bolitho in like vein described the story as "one of the deepest manifestations of sheer world despair since 'The City of Dreadful Night.'"[9]

Although there are grounds for some differences of opinion regarding the meaning of "The Golden Honeymoon," it is nevertheless difficult to understand how the story could have provoked such extremely divergent views as these. While it is hardly a warmly sympathetic piece of "human interest writing," it is surely not at the other extreme, a "smashing indictment of 'happy marriage'" or an expression of "sheer world despair." The first position overlooks the spiritual barrenness of the old man and woman whose trip through life has not been one of growth and development but only a time schedule, a fact symbolized by the railroad timetable the old man monotonously recites in his monologue. Despite having journeyed through all the stations of life from youth to old age, the two old people have failed to develop wisdom or self-reliance; therefore, their thoughts are turned outward and their attention fixed on the banalities of daily existence. Viewed thus, the story is an ironic commentary on the empty, nearly meaningless journey countless people make through life.

But what the second position—that of viewing the story as wholly pessimistic—disregards is that for the old couple the trip through life has not lacked purpose or meaning, though it may seem so to the reader. Despite their senseless quarrel or their indulgence in petty grievances of various sorts, they have a warm attachment for each other; and if the things which give them pleasure are as trifling as those which provoke irritation, the point is that they still have pleasures: Mother enjoys meeting people at the "Chiropodist's," and the old man glories in the speech he makes before the New York–New Jersey Society. While the characters Lardner used permitted him to dramatize the battle of the sexes with a couple advanced in age, the story is also a commentary on old age as well as on marriage. It shows what age does to people: it dries up such inner resources as they may have had to begin with, it makes them crotchety and garrulous, and it causes them to become absorbed in the trivialities of life. Nevertheless, the story makes no indictment of elderly people of the kind—a very typical kind—the couple represent; it simply presents them as they are.

III   *Eccentric Athletes*

The dreary conventionality of the old couple in "Golden Honeymoon" stands in dramatic contrast to the eccentricity of B. (for "Buster") Elliott, the main character of "My Roomy," which is not only the most unusual story in *How to Write Short Stories*, but one of the most unusual stories Lardner wrote. Elliott is a busher from Michigan playing with the Chicago Cubs to earn enough money to marry his hometown girl friend. Elliott knows or cares nothing about fielding, but at bat "he sure can bust 'em." He lives up to his first name, however, by "busting" more things than baseballs—a window through which he throws a water pitcher; the sleep of his successive roommates by running the water in the bathtub or turning on the lights to shave at midnight; a card game in his room by raucously singing "Silver Threads among the Gold" at the top of his lungs. Moreover, he "busts" up ball games either by hitting winning runs or by deliberately striking out on critical plays.

Forced to conclude that Elliott is a hopeless case, the team manager sells him to Atlanta; and when Elliott learns this fact, he comes to the room he shares with the player who is the narrator of the story and "sits down on the bed and begins to cry like a baby. 'No series dough for me,' he blubbers, 'and no weddin' bells! My girl'll die when she hears about it'" (212). But he does not cry long:

> Pretty soon he goes up to the lookin'-glass and stares at himself for five minutes. Then, all of a sudden, he hauls off and takes a wallop at his reflection in the glass. Naturally he smashed the glass all to pieces and he cut his hand somethin' awful.
>
> Without lookin' at it he come over to me and says: "Well, good-by, sport!"—and holds out his other hand to shake. When I starts to shake with him he smears his bloody hand all over my map. Then he laughed like a wild man and run out 'o the room and out o' the hotel (212-13).

But not even this gruesome "bust" is his last one: returning to his home town instead of going to Atlanta, he finds his girl friend married to a drugstore operator and tries to kill the pair with a baseball bat: ". . . but I guess I did not meet 'em square," he writes his former roomy. "They tell me they are both alive yet, which I did not mean 'em to be" (215-16). At the end, having thus made a "bust" of life, as well as of his career and everything else, he is locked up, waiting to be taken to an asylum.

Had Lardner written "My Roomy" late in his career, about the time he wrote "Mamma" and "Poodle," which deal with mentally deranged characters, its morbidity would hardly surprise us. Actually published May 9, 1914, it is the second regular piece of fiction Lardner produced, being preceded only by the first installment of *You Know Me Al.* No other character Lardner depicted between 1914 and 1924 is so violent as Elliott except Midge Kelly, but there is really little comparison between the two other than that both are "busters"; for Elliott is partly irrational, whereas Midge Kelly is calculatingly vicious; and Elliott is presented sympathetically despite his homicidal tendencies, while Kelly is made the object of contempt. By thus differing from any other characters Lardner presented during the period, Elliott prompts a question: What significance are we to attach to him? Was Lardner's purpose merely that of drawing the portrait of an eccentric player, perhaps of one he had encountered himself? Or does the character have a deeper significance?

Howard Webb, Jr., who regards "My Roomy" as Lardner's "most revealing story," views Elliott as a character seeking self-definition—one engaged in trying to establish an image of himself (in contrast to Jack Keefe and Midge Kelly, who are engaged in maintaining the images they have already formed). To Webb, Elliott's eccentricities prevent his entering "the world of normality" represented by his roommate, a world Elliott curses by smearing his bloody hand on the roommate's face. Hence, Webb sees the fundamental point of the story as "the horror and terror of being perpetually and irrevocably incommunicado."[10]

Although this interpretation is plausible, it leaves room for questioning whether the emphasis of the story falls as much on the "horror and terror" of being "incommunicado" as it does on the tragedy of a person trapped by the repeated collision of his self-created narcissistic world of illusion with the world of actuality. Elliott combines the defect of incomplete understanding or half-knowledge with an overweening self-confidence, and the story shows what fateful consequences can result from this dangerous combination of traits when it is untempered either by humility or the desire for fuller knowledge. Elliott's egotism leads him to rush into both the serious and "play" games of life with unwarranted assurance that he holds the winning hand, and the result is that he impales himself on the sharp reality of actual circumstances which his ignorance has caused him to disregard or fail to anticipate.

Lardner nowhere makes Elliott's predicament in life clearer than through the card game in the story. When Elliott is asked whether or not he knows how to play poker, he brashly says, "They's nothin' I can't do!," and gets into the game with two dollars he borrows from his roommate. By sheer luck, he wins several pots but soon loses all his money betting on a small straight which he correctly recognizes as a good hand but mistakenly believes is the top poker hand. When he seeks another stake to continue his wild playing, his roommate tells him that he is "barred from the game for life," to which Elliott replies: "Well, . . . if I can't play no more . . . you fellers will have to get out o' this room." When his roommate chides him for "bustin'" up "ball games in the afternoon and poker games at night," Elliott tells him: "That's my business—bustin' things" (202).

Just as Elliott overvalued his poker hand, so he overvalues all the other "hands" he holds. He believes hitting ability is the only thing which counts in baseball, that singing consists of mere volume of sound alone, and that he can destroy the letters his girl friend sends him without reading them because they always say the same thing. But least of all does he grant to others the right also to be "busters"—his roommates to leave him when they find his conduct intolerable, the team manager to fire him for deliberately losing a game, his girl to throw him over for a man she likes better. When he is finally "busted" completely in the collision of his self-created world of illusion with the world of reality, he makes a violent protest against both worlds: against the first by striking at the reflection of himself in the mirror and against the second by attempting to murder the couple he believes has betrayed him. In both cases, he inflicts more damage on himself than on the objects of his defeat; he ends up committed to an asylum, literally barred from all the games he has sought to play, as he was barred from poker.

This interesting story, however, raises one final question: Did Lardner intend the reader to view Elliott as an insane person or merely as a highly eccentric one? Elliott's teammates regard him as "just a plain nut" and his behavior seems to confirm their judgment, but in the end a jury declares him insane. Still, the indirection of Lardner's method permitted him to cloak the issue of Elliott's sanity with ambiguity. The reader knows only what the narrator reports about Elliott, and the story provides no grounds for regarding the jury which tried Elliott as less fallible than juries usually are. Had Lardner not made it possible for the reader to view Elliott's behavior partly as that of an irrational man, the story would lack plausibility; at the same time had he presented the character as obviously deranged, the story would lose significance as a commentary on human beings and human conduct. Hence, Lardner presented Elliott as a markedly eccentric character—one neither wholly rational nor wholly irrational.

Several other characters depicted in the volume also have unusual twists to their personalities, but none is so extremely eccentric as Elliott. Frank X. Farrell of "Alibi Ike," for example, is a ballplayer who simply refuses to admit publicly—perhaps even to himself—that a plain fact is a plain fact, even when the one at issue reflects credit on him. Thus, he offers an alibi for his every action, never pulling a play "good or bad, on or off field, without apologizin' for it" (81). Despite his nearly losing his girl when she overhears him giving his teammates an alibi for having become engaged to her, Farrell's harmless peculiarity actually endears him to people instead of alienating him from them, as did Elliott's. Another character, Burke, of "A Frame-Up," a naturally gifted prizefighter, has the peculiarity that he will hit his opponents with his full strength only when seeking to gain the approval of a girl; his manager, therefore, has to invent a mythical admirer in order to make him fight at his best. Art Graham of "Harmony" is a baseball player so obsessed with "harmonizing" that he gladly yields his position on the team to a rookie who is talented both in singing and playing baseball. Still another baseball story, "Horseshoes," presents two players who are opposites in that one is lucky and the other unlucky in his playing, but in a major game the wheel of fortune finally turns and reverses their roles.

The characters in the two remaining stories, "The Facts" and "A Caddy's Diary," however, have no special quirks of personality to distinguish them from their class and kind. "The Facts" is a comic story about a young man who gets drunk while shopping for Christmas presents and insults his fiancée and the stuffy members of her family with ludicrously inappropriate gifts. "A Caddy's Diary," one of the better stories in the collection, deals with a sixteen-year-old golf caddy who critically watches his golfers sell their souls by cheating to win petty prizes; but at the end the caddy awakens to the realization that by assisting them in their cheating he is selling his own soul for mere tips and smiles.

IV *Significance of How to Write Short Stories*

The ten stories in *How to Write Short Stories*, then, present an interesting variety of characters and themes, but at least four of them are mediocre in quality. Perhaps the poorest one in the collection is "A Frame-Up," which is inferior to many of the uncollected stories Lardner wrote during this period. While "The Facts," "Horseshoes," and "Harmony" are amusing, they nevertheless are trivial pieces in comparison with "The Golden Honeymoon," "Some Like Them Cold," and "Champion." Regardless of the unevenness of the quality of the stories or of the fact that Lardner's facetious preface and notes seemed to invite critics and readers alike to view *How to Write Short Stories* as a humorous work, nearly all critics recognized the merit of the better stories in the volume and saw that they were serious works of fiction rather than of humor. The reviews of the volume were so favorable in fact that Lardner expressed to Fitzgerald the fear that the readers might think he "was having an affair with some of the critics."[11]

Scoff as Lardner might at the important new role assigned him by the critics, he thereafter was regarded as a major—by some critics as *the* major—satirist of his era, being frequently compared with Sinclair Lewis, to the latter's disadvantage. In his review of the volume, Edmund Wilson, for example, said: "You have to read the whole of a novel of Lewis to find out that there is anything remarkable about it; but there is scarcely a paragraph of Lardner's which, in its irony both fresh and morose, does not convey somehow the sense of a distinguished aloof intelligence. And he has shown an unexcelled, a perhaps unrivalled, mastery of what since the publication of Mencken's book, has come to be known as the American language."[12] As might be expected, the last-mentioned quality—Lardner's ability to handle the idiom, to make his characters reveal themselves—was the one critics praised most consistently. To cite one example, Robert Littell noted that Lardner's "extra-ordinary gift" was that he knew "the difference between letting his characters talk, and making them do so."[13] But this critic, as did others, recognized that it was Lardner's understanding of his characters, his knowledge of the way their minds worked, which gave his idiom its authenticity.

CHAPTER 5

The Peak Years:
The Love Nest and *Round Up*

AFTER slackening his production of short stories in the early 1920's and even passing through an idle period in 1923 and 1924 when he wrote none at all, Lardner resumed writing them in 1925 with fresh energy and a new seriousness. Within the twelve months from March, 1925, to March, 1926, he published nine, all of which soon reappeared in *Love Nest* (1926), a collection of far better overall quality than *How to Write Short Stories*. During the next three years, he published twenty-one more, sixteen of which he included in *Round Up* (1929), together with the nineteen he had already reprinted in his two earlier collections. From 1925 to 1929, he published thirty new stories, or an average of more than seven per year, thus attaining a rate of production he had exceeded in only one other four-year period, that from 1914 to 1918. Although he chose to reprint less than half of the stories of the earlier period, he reprinted all but five of those written from 1925 to early 1929.

Lardner displayed sound critical judgment in choosing to reprint as many of the stories as he did; for even if some are little more than character sketches and a few others are quite insignificant works, their average quality is high. A round dozen of them approximate or match the excellence of "Some Like Them Cold," "The Golden Honeymoon," and "Champion." So far as separate short stories are concerned, *The Love Nest* collection and the sixteen new stories in *Round Up* show Lardner at the height of his artistic powers. He had written some of his best stories before 1925 and would yet write a few more interesting, though not superior, ones after publishing *Round Up*, but he wrote most of his best stories in this four-year period.

As the fruit of Lardner's peak years, these stories display a number of characteristics which distinguish them from his earlier ones. First, there is a difference in the kind of subject matter and characters treated. A majority of the twenty-eight stories written before 1925 deal with the world of sports, but only two of the twenty-five collected stories, "Women" and "Hurry Kane," and only one of five uncollected ones, "The Venomous Viper of the Volga," deal with athletes and sports. By the late 1920's Lardner had evidently gone beyond the kind of material on which his early fame had been based, preferring instead to depict a highly diversified assortment of nonathletic American types—mismatched married couples, Broadway show people, inhabitants of small towns, bridge-players, young girls, and the like.

Second, there is a difference in technique. At last fulfilling his desire to vary his habitual mode of writing first-person dialect stories, Lardner used the third person more frequently than he had at first; and though in every case he made the characters use the kinds of language their real life counterparts would use, he wrote many of the stories in "straight" English. Moreover, with few exceptions, the stories are shorter and more economically written than are most of his earlier ones. Even though Lardner brushed aside the critical acclaim *How to Write Short Stories* had brought him, it may have influenced him to work with more conscious artistry than ever before. Finally, as the result of the deepened critical attitude he developed during the decade, there is a difference in the tone of the stories. Some are funny—"Zone of Quiet," "Contract," and "Dinner," for example—but not a single one is purely humorous, like some of his earlier ones, and several of the best ones are decidedly satirical rather than humorous.

In sum, these twenty-five stories from *Love Nest* and *Round Up* are the solid core of Lardner's best work, on which his reputation as a serious literary artist must rest. This chapter will first survey the themes and characters he treated in these stories, examine next their style and technique, and finally evaluate them as works of art.

I Themes and Characters

No single theme presented in the stories drew more serious attention from Lardner than that of marital discord—the splitting apart of a man and woman whose marriage goes on the rocks or becomes an agony to be endured because of incompatibility. Lardner's concern with this theme, not merely in this group of stories but also in much of his other fiction, led Clifton Fadiman to describe him as "the epic recorder of the Great American Bicker."[1] Without knowing that Lardner had formed an ideal of harmonious family relationships during his youth in Niles and later adhered to it in his own family life, one would be at a loss to explain his persistent concern with bickering and unhappily married couples. He was, however, perpetually concerned with the difference between the real and the ideal, between the actual state of human affairs and the happier state they might enjoy. To him marital discord was one of the more common and tragic manifestations of the departure of human behavior from an ideal standard; it was a dramatic example of the inability of people to get along with one another.

Whatever the case, four of the most severely critical stories in this group—"Love Nest," "Ex Parte," "Now and Then," and "Anniversary"—deal with incompatible married couples; four others place a secondary emphasis on jangled marital relationships. "The Love Nest" depicts the tragic irony of a marriage based on money and self-interest instead of on the firmer grounds of mutual respect and affection. Lou Gregg, as wealthy as he is pompous and vain, marries a promising movie star because he wants a handsome woman in his gaudy mansion to bear him pretty children. In her turn, Celia Sayles, the young star, marries the "great man," neither because she desires to add the décor of her beauty to his other possessions nor to bear his children, but because she expects him to make her a famous movie star. When he refuses to permit her to have a career, she finds herself writhing in the trap she has closed on herself: "Well, he's made me all right; he's made me a chronic mother and it's a wonder I've got any looks left," she bitterly complains to Bartlett, the newspaper reporter in the story (*LN*, 23). Having become a thing—"I'm just like his big diamond or his cars or his horses" (*LN*, 24)—she must ironically act a part, pretending to be the happy, loving wife, while loathing her husband with all her soul and taking refuge in secret drinking. Her husband, "great man" that he is, has an unbridled faith in the power of money: ". . . no amount of money is too much to spend on a home," he tells Bartlett. "I mean it's a good investment if it tends to make your family proud and satisfied with their home. I mean every nickel I've spent here is like so much insurance; it insures me of a happy wife and family" (*LN*, 4). In short, the vulgar Gregg places the same value on money that the Duke in Browning's "My Last Duchess" placed on his ancient lineage and, like the Duke, Gregg's every thought turns on self-interest.

"Ex Parte," a story fully as powerful as "Love Nest," presents a different kind of situation, the more common one of a marriage which ends disastrously as the result of the couple's completely different tastes. The man, a middle-class vulgarian, loves bright, new, shiny things, while his wife Florence has a passion for old things—country houses converted from antique barns and period furniture. Before the marriage and without consulting his bride-to-be, the man purchases a house in the city, "all new and shiny and a bargain if you ever saw one" (*RU*, 212), filled with ornate, overstuffed furniture which the previous owners had permitted a furniture store to select for them. When he brings his bride into the monstrosity, he is both provoked and mystified by the tears she sheds, being unable to understand why she is not thrilled by the house and its furnishings, since in his view they represent near-perfection. It is inconceivable to him that his wife can admire the barn her friends the Dwans have remodeled into a house and filled with early American furniture, pieces such as a maple "low-boy," a "dough-trough" table, a "Dutch" chest. He jeers at her admiration for such "junk," as he calls it, until she bursts out in anger and tells him that she hates his house and everything in it: "It's too new! Everything shines! I loathe new things!" (*RU*, 219). Thereupon, the husband goes out, has a few drinks, and returns home with a blowtorch and an ax, which he spitefully uses to "antique" the furniture his wife finds objectionable, an act of childish anger which wrecks both his furniture and his marriage.

At first thought, it would appear that the husband is the chief offender in this case, but closer analysis shows that the woman is far from blameless. While her tastes are more refined than her husband's, she is as selfishly insistent on them as her husband is on his; and she makes no more attempt than her husband to seek a workable compromise. "Ex Parte," however, is not a fictionized sociological treatise; it is a work of art which touches human problems of far greater depth than the foreground issue of unhappy marital relations. No one has described the real meaning of the story better than Jarvis A. Thurston, who said:

> Both the husband and wife in "Ex Parte" are insistent upon having each other conform to their different sets of acquired values (each feels that his or her tastes represents a universal truth), and the more important human relationship is destroyed in less than two months by their egocentric views of the world. And the relationship between the teller (i.e., the husband) and his wife, the story implies, is in microcosm what we see in human relationships on a much grander scale, between social class and social class, between race and race, between nation and nation. Everyone is queer except me.[2]

By contrast, "Now and Then" presents a somewhat milder, though no less telling, treatment of the breakdown of the relationship between a husband and wife. The breakdown occurs in the interval between a first trip the couple makes to Nassau and a second one, three years later. On the first, which is a seven months' delayed honeymoon, the husband devotes his whole attention to the wife, wanting to spend every minute in privacy with her, taking her to an exclusive beach where no other man will see her in a bathing suit, and even objecting to her writing to an old girl friend about the belated honeymoon. His narrow-minded jealousy and overpossessiveness lead the simple-minded wife to believe that she is forever enshrined in his heart as an object of adoration, so that she is puzzled by his treatment of her on the second trip. He finds excuses to leave her alone, urges her to go out with another man, reminds her that she can while away her time writing her girl friend about her troubles, and finally sends her home while he remains in Nassau to continue his pursuit of another woman.

Just as the discordant marital relation in "Ex Parte" carries the overtone of a universal issue, so it does in "Now and Then." However much the boorish, egocentric husband is at fault, the wife is also again at fault. Her trouble is that she stands still in time, quite literally living in the "then" of the years before, not merely on her second trip to Nassau, but on her first as well, where she faithfully maintains her tie with her old friend Esther. By contrast the husband lives entirely in the "now," at first idolizing his wife and then turning from her to pursue another woman, as a child turns impatiently from an old toy to a new one when time brings a change of mood. The breach between "Then and Now"—Lardner's first title for the story—which separates this couple is one which separates man and man as frequently as it does man and woman.

"Anniversary," the fourth story using unhappy marital relations as a major foreground theme, presents yet another type of polarity—that of dullness and excitement. The story contrasts the boring situation of a woman married to a dull, sedate, "safe" husband with the exciting one of a woman married to a veritable hell-raiser and wife-beater. The life of the first wife is so drearily monotonous that she nearly loses her mind; that of the second is filled with dramatic tensions and constant uncertainties, though she would trade places with no other woman because she knows her husband is devoted to her despite his predilection for getting drunk, carrying on flirtations with other women, and occasionally poking her in the eye. Such emotionalism as the dull husband may have had to begin with has evaporated, and for him marriage has become merely a routine habit—as have his reading aloud to his wife from the newspaper and his repeating the same stories to her over and over again. The rambunctious husband is a creature of temperament who lives with his feelings on the surface and thus constantly places the marriage tie under stress. Even though the story implies that the wife of the hell-raiser has a better marital bargain than the woman with the dull husband, the issue, nevertheless, obviously is not which mode of marital existence—and more generally, of existence in life—is preferable. Rather it is basically the same issue which is behind the *old-new* contrast of "Ex Parte" and the *then-now* contrast of "Now and Then": namely, that, being as they are, people seek to impose their egocentric view of the world on others, so that conflict and unhappiness inevitably result.

It may be noted further that the real source of the unhappiness in "The Love Nest" is that the woman has been unable to impose her egocentric desire for a career on her husband but instead has become the victim of his egocentric desire for a feminine orna-ment and bearer of children. Thus, though the four stories dealing with unhappily married couples approach the problem in quite different ways, they make essentially the same statement about it, a larger issue than marriage itself being at stake in each case. The theme of discordant marriage, therefore, provided Lardner with convenient material for dramatizing the universal problem of jangled human relationships, which is one of the most persistent themes running through his work.

Despite Lardner's repeated concern with unhappily married couples, he nevertheless presented many who were apparently happily mated, a fact less often noted by commentators than his concern with mismatched couples. Both the city couple and the country couple in "Reunion," for example, are well-mated—or at least they share the same interests. The city couple likes bridge, golf, and drinking; the country couple, gardening, sight-seeing, and "Abie's Irish Rose," which they see time and again. So, too, the couple in "Mr. and Mrs. Fix-It," a pair of meddlers who share the same tastes, and seem as well suited to each other as the couple on whom they seek to impose their views. Again, the couple in "Old Folks' Christmas" is a particularly devoted one, and Lardner's portrait even verges on sentimentality. Still, when the marriage partners are not in conflict with each other, they are in conflict with other persons—sometimes with other members of their family, as in "Reunion" and "Old Folks' Christmas," but most typically with other couples, as in "Mr. and Mrs. Fix-It," "Liberty Hall," and "Contract." The conflict between a harmonious couple and an antagonistic couple usually arises from the same source as that between individual husbands and wives: the desire of the opposing couple to impose its own views on the united pair. Lardner's fictional world is a world of unending strife.

An even larger number of this group of stories deals with the general theme of man and woman in conquest of each other—that is, with marriage in view—than with that of their harmonious or discordant relationships after the conquest has resulted in marriage. "I Can't Breathe," for example, presents a young girl so much in love with love that she is nearly hysterical: she finds males so readily available and the problem of choosing among them so difficult that she becomes engaged to three simultaneously and then throws over the whole lot for an old flame who shows up at the end. The satire in this story is quite gentle; Lardner obviously intended the reader to be amused by, not critical of, this eighteen-year-old girl's breathless emotionalism, which he caught to perfection in every line of the story.

But Lardner depicted sympathetically neither the nurse in "Zone of Quiet" nor the vain woman tourist in "Travelogue"; for they are both shallow-brained, talkative females who delude themselves about their charms while they cast slurs on their quieter, more intelligent, if less beautiful, girl friends. In both cases, as in several other stories not included in this group, the vanity-ridden, talkative women appear to be making headway with the men of their choice, only to be rudely jolted in the end to discover that the quiet ones have silently stolen away the prizes—such as they are; for very often it appears that the quiet girl might have done better to tiptoe away alone. As a case in point, the girl who wins the man in "Travelogue" is surely doomed to go through life responding to her husband's invitation to peer into his mouth at the vacancy left by the loss of his rotten molar or offering him condolences for similar grievances.

Still another story, "Dinner," presents not one but two shallow-minded females between whom an eligible bachelor finds himself seated at a dinner party. The zany on one side is unable to stop talking, even though she must reuse the same limited stock of conversational topics; the one on the other side is unable to complete a thought so that her conversation is gibberish: " 'Three of us girls—I think it was four winters—it was three winters ago. One night we went—it's the Holy Rollers—honestly they do the craziest—a man told us they were just—but I couldn't believe it, they were so—I think—Have you ever been there Mr. Burton?' " (RU, 144-45). Though "Dinner" is better described as a character sketch than as a short story, Lardner presents in it his most caustic indictment of the brainless tongue-wagger, a type which must have grated on his nerves.

In contrast to "Zone of Quiet," "Travelogue," and "Contrast," wherein vain women are made the targets of satire, "Women" and "Hurry Kane" satirize the vain behavior of men in their relationships with women. In both stories, the men characters are simply woman-crazy. In the first, a baseball player has lost his regular position on the team and become a bench-warmer as the result of his unfortunate involvements with women, whom he pretends to hate at the very moment he lets his eyes rest admiringly on a pretty girl in the grandstands. In "Hurry Kane," a talented rookie pitcher, not content with the devoted girl friend he already has, nearly wrecks his baseball career by permitting a second one to influence him to accept a bribe. Further, in "Man Not Overboard," a show-girl almost drives a successful novelist to suicide, and in "There are Smiles" a burly New York traffic cop falls for a pretty girl who is later killed in a traffic mishap.

Although several of the stories dealing with the battle of the sexes theme are comparable in merit to "Some Like Them Cold"— notably, "Zone of Quiet," "I Can't Breathe," and "Travelogue"— most of them rank among the poorest of the twenty-five. Perhaps such stories, more than any other type Lardner wrote, show that even at the height of his career he never lost sight of his mass-circulation magazine audience, one craving stories about young love. Even so, he never stooped to writing the conventional boy-meets-girl stories which filled the other pages of the same magazines in which he published his; to the contrary, he invariably poked fun at his romantic couples, if not always severely, at least mildly. Lardner satirized the stereotyped idea of young love as he had satirized other stereotypes, such as the athlete and the businessman.

Turning next to a different group of characters and to a different theme, one finds that a number of the stories in this group deal with meddlers of various sorts, persons who bring displeasure if not actual suffering and real damage to others because of malicious or witless interference in their affairs. The most outstanding example of the malicious meddler and of the most hurtful form of meddling is presented by Jim Kendall of "Haircut," a character almost as vicious as Midge Kelly. He meddles with the lives of his wife and children, not merely by sending them to see a circus they have no money to attend, but more seriously by letting them nearly starve to death. He meddles in the lives of Doc Stair and Julia Gregg in the attempt to break up their budding romance; he even disturbs the lives of people he has never seen, or will ever see, by sending them anonymous cards designed to bring husbands and wives into conflict. He meets his death as the result of his meddling—appropriately, at the hands of a person who, though a half-wit, possesses the human decency Kendall lacks—and he richly deserves his fate.

The practical joker in "The Maysville Minstrel" also deserves, but fails to receive, a heavy penalty for his interference in the life of a poverty-stricken, simple-minded employee of a small-town gas company. The practical joker, Charley Roberts, having discovered that Stephen Gale, the employee, writes verses, though of a ludicrously pathetic kind, persuades Gale to lend him some of his poems to show a newspaperman, telling him that he may receive as much as a dollar a line for them. Then Roberts sends Gale a bogus letter from an "editor" offering to buy the poems, whereupon Gale resigns his job, intending to support his wife and children with his verse-writing. Soon discovering that he is the victim of a practical joke, Gale manages to regain his old job and resume his futile existence on starvation wages. Thus, unlike "Haircut," the practical joker in "The Maysville Minstrel" pays no penalty for his meddling, because his victim is helpless and unable to retaliate.

The meddling in "Mr. and Mrs. Fix-It" and "Liberty Hall" takes a less cruel form than that in "Haircut" and "The Maysville Minstrel," but it is even more significant because a more common type and thus more likely to be encountered than is practical joking. Though it seems well-intentioned and therefore a witless or thoughtless form of intrusion in the lives of others, the meddling in both stories takes the form of one couple's minding another couple's business. In "Mr. and Mrs. Fix-It," Belle and Tom Stevens, the "fix-it" couple, seek to direct the lives and habits of another husband and wife by telling them where to live, where to purchase their clothes, what kind to purchase, which trains to ride, where to go on vacation trips, and so on. In "Liberty Hall," a famous composer and his wife temporarily become the prisoners of an overzealous host and hostess who take the couple to their estate to let them relax and enjoy themselves and then at every turn impose their tastes and viewpoints on them.

These stories imply that this form of meddling has its source in the selfish gratification of the ego, in the desire of one person to demonstrate to another the superiority of his knowledge, judgment, and taste, rather than in the desire to aid a fellow human being. Thus, it constitutes a breach of good manners, particularly when it becomes overt criticism, a viewpoint Lardner expressed clearly in another story, "Contract." There, through a magazine editor who might well be his mouthpiece, Lardner took note of the predilection of people to criticize others but to resent criticism themselves: "It's a conviction of most bridge players, and some golf players, that God sent them into the world to teach. At that, what they tell you isn't intended for your edification and future good. It's just a way of announcing 'I'm smart and you're a lunkhead'. And to my mind it's a revelation of bad manners and bad sportsmanship. If I ask somebody what I did wrong, that's different" (*RU*, 131). Fed up with the criticism of his bridge-playing, the character first forces his critics to acknowledge that they believe they had his best interest at heart in criticizing his playing; then, with satanic glee, he sets about correcting their table manners and grammar, whereupon he is asked to leave. The point of the story is that the same principle is involved in both types of criticism, one type being as crudely offensive as the other. The story thus dramatizes the old adage that what "I" do is right and what "you" do is wrong.

Besides showing how human relationships become twisted as the result of people's desire to impose their egocentric view of the world on others—as in the stories dealing with discordant marriages—or by the desire to control the lives of others and thus gratify their vanities—as in the stories dealing with serious types of meddlers such as Jim Kendall and Charley Roberts and less serious but more common ones such as "Mr. and Mrs. Fix-It" —Lardner treated in several stories yet another of the obstacles to human harmony and decency. It is the obstacle of self-obsession and consequently of self-delusion, expressed through characters who have not a jot of regard to spare for others, the only pity they can feel being self-pity. Thus, they immolate all human decency on the altar of the false image they have created of themselves and which they worship above all else. Unless it be Midge Kelly of "Champion," no character Lardner created better exemplifies this self-obsession than Conrad Green of "A Day with Conrad Green." Green regards the death of his underpaid secretary as a personal affront to himself, as a thoughtless act bringing Green serious inconvenience. And when he is caught trying to pass off a stolen idea to a libretto writer, he is indignant, not at himself, but at the person who gave him the idea. He is reduced to deep gloom by being forced to purchase an expensive show advertisement in a paper to avoid public exposé of his unpaid gambling debts. But self-pity really overcomes him when his wife inadvertently tricks him into giving her a necklace he has intended to present to his mistress, who then withholds her "love" until he can get another. Except for being able to cheat the widow of his secretary out of the secretary's last pay check, Green has a day which is a total failure. To Conrad Green, the whole world seems against him—"To hell with all of them!" he says—but his jangled relationships with his fellow men and women are created entirely by the egotism of his own rotten personality.

That the fatality of Conrad Green's self-obsession is that he lives a lie to himself and before the world is made clear by another story, "Rhythm." In it, a tune thief and his lyric-stealing partner are a successful song-writing team as long as they face the truth and admit that they are what they are. But the lyric writer breaks up the partnership because his wife considers it unethical to steal other people's ideas. The tune writer in his turn becomes the victim of self-delusion when a critic praises his work and spurs him to undertake musical compositions beyond his abilities. Both nearly starve until economic necessity compels each to come to his senses: one admits that he is not capable of creating original compositions; the other, that he has no capacity to create lyrics without borrowing ideas. Thus, although both characters are guilty of a type of dishonesty, they are at least honest about their dishonesty, and it is pretty clear that Lardner could view an honest thief with more complacency than he could a thoroughly dishonest one such as Conrad Green.

Two other stories, "Sun Cured" and "Old Folks' Christmas," also deal with thoroughly self-obsessed characters. Ernie Fretts in the first story is wholly concerned with the selfish pleasures of drinking, gambling, and having fun; and the trip he takes to Florida for his health at the suggestion of the secretary who manages his insurance agency serves merely to provide a new locale for his self-indulgence. The second story, "Old Folks' Christmas" presents two children, home from school for the Christmas holidays, who are so entirely intent on their own pleasures and friends that they hardly see their fond, overindulgent parents, except to demand that the parents exchange the expensive presents given them for different but equally expensive ones.

Thus, both stories deal with thoughtless characters absorbed in pleasure and self-indulgence, the bachelor in "Sun Cured" damaging nobody but himself, but the children in "Old Folks' Christmas" cruelly wounding the feelings of those who have their interests at heart. Still, there are no implications in either story that the characters—Fretts on the one hand, the children on the other—are incurably self-obsessed: as was true of the lyric writer in "Rhythm," time and changed circumstances may dispel their total self-absorption. But not so that of such characters as Conrad Green, Midge Kelly, and Lou Gregg, who possess such virulent forms of egomania that they are doomed to carry it with them to their graves, as did Jim Kendall. Few Lardner characters fail to display some degree of self-centeredness, but without exception all his most thoroughly despicable ones are self-centered to an extreme degree. They view the world through false self-images which permit them to convert their vices into virtues and trample roughshod over others—or at least attempt to do so—without the least tinge of compassion for their victims. Lardner was able to view some forms of egotism dispassionately or even sympathetically, as Jack Keefe and many other characters illustrate; but clearly he regarded self-obsession of the extreme, ruthless type that Green, Kendall, and Kelly represent as a tragically hurtful evil.

The foregoing discussion has made no attempt to mention all the themes or different character types Lardner used in the fiction of this four-year period when his artistry reached full development. Those mentioned, however, are the most representative and dominant ones. Just as in his earlier fiction he had already presented nearly every character type included in the stories of this period, so he had already introduced in former stories most of the themes he used; but never before had he centered his fiction so consistently on the issue of disturbed, confused, or tangled human relationships as he did in this period. Despite the fact that some of the characters are victors or that others are apparently well satisfied with their lot in life, most of them are unhappy and engaged in strife with others, seeking somehow to make their will prevail. There are individuals in conflict with those around them because of seeking to make the world conform to the distortion of false self-images. There are husbands in conflict with wives because one desires to impose on the other his or her egocentric view of the world. There are married couples in conflict with each other because one pair thoughtlessly or maliciously intrudes into the other's affairs to demonstrate an imagined superiority of knowledge and taste, and so on. Regardless of whether the conflicts have highly serious consequences or result only in momentary irritations or minor disappointments, they all have their basis in some form of egotism.

II *Style and Narrative Technique*

In terms of his development as a writer, no phase of the fictional method Lardner displayed in this group of stories is more significant or interesting than his handling of the narrative point of view. Now that he had at last succeeded in breaking away from his fixed practice of writing in the first person, he achieved unusual skill and variety in writing both from the limited third-person and the fully omniscient-author points of view. Further, while he continued writing in the first person, he demonstrated greater variety in its use also, none of his first-person stories of this period producing the impression, as some of his earlier ones do, that they could have been narrated more effectively from a different angle. In fact, in every case, regardless of whether he used a form of the first or of the third person, he narrated all these stories, the poorer ones as well as the better ones, from a point of view which seems to be the only one fully appropriate to the intention and effect of the particular story. Lardner had been a conscientious craftsman from the beginning, but in this period he became a highly self-conscious one, welding the structural elements of his stories into tightly coordinated designs wherein every detail, however small, plays a functional role. For Lardner, as for other story writers, the narrative method employed became one of the main controlling principles of his story designs, determining both their organization and style.

"The Love Nest" provides an excellent illustration of Lardner's use of the limited third person and also shows how skillfully and economically he could interweave the elements of theme, plot, character, setting, and style to produce a desired effect—in this story a highly ironic one. The action of "The Love Nest" unfolds in four major scenes, with a minor character, the reporter Bartlett, serving as a focal point for what the two main characters, Lou and Celia Gregg, say about themselves and each other. Gregg first talks to Bartlett alone; then both of the Greggs talk to him, and before him, to each other, where on the surface they appear to be a loving and devoted couple; and in the next two scenes, Celia Gregg talks to Bartlett alone, where he (as well as the reader) learns the truth about the Greggs's disastrous marriage. Enough hints are given to make it clear that Bartlett sees the Greggs for what they are, but he provides no center of consciousness through which the reader is made to comprehend the action, as might be the case had Henry James written the story. Bartlett does, however, represent the position from which the two main characters must be viewed; and the reader is stationed with him, as at an observation post, hearing the characters talk and seeing what they do. Thus, with the descriptive and explanatory comment being held to the bare minimum needed to introduce the characters and make the transitions between scenes, Lardner presents the story through dialogue, much as if it were a play acted out before the reader. This restrained, dramatic handling of the characters and situations enhances the ironic effect of the story: the reader is made to see objectively that the "love nest" is a hate nest.

Lardner narrated "A Day with Conrad Green" in a similar manner, except that he made the main character, Conrad Green, the focal point of the dialogue and more fully staged the character with introductory comment before beginning the dialogue than he had done in "The Love Nest." Once he got the story underway, however, he used little additional explanatory comment, and the story unfolds objectively and dramatically through the dialogue between Green and the numerous minor characters who successively enter and leave his office, their entrances and exits being similar to those of characters in a play. Each scene of the story, as in "Champion," shows the main character from a different angle, progressively enlarging and intensifying his personality, so that in the end he stands exposed in the full breadth and depth of his loathesomeness. Further, the scheme of the story permitted Lardner to use naturally and logically a large miscellaneous assortment of minor characters, some being the victims of Green's cupidity and meanness, but others being victors over him or at least seeking to prey on him as he preys on others. Through these characters, good or bad alike, Lardner suggested the milieu of Broadway show business in which Green operates and used them as a backdrop against which he could more effectively display Green's rottenness.

The method Lardner used in this story, that of staging the main character with introductory comment and thereafter developing the story primarily through dialogue, is one he commonly used, as in such stories as "The Maysville Minstrel," "Reunion," "Man Not Overboard," and "Anniversary." In others, such as "Contract" and "Rhythm," the presence of the omniscient author is strongly felt; and in a few, of which "There are Smiles" is the best illustration, Lardner even adopts a chatty, confidential tone, the kind of it's-between-me-and-you tone that O. Henry was fond of using. At the other extreme, however, are a number of stories—"Zone of Quiet," "Sun Cured," and "Dinner" being the most notable ones among them—in which the presence of an omniscient author, if sensed at all, is felt even less than in "The Love Nest" and "A Day with Conrad Green." These stories use interior monologues, where the main characters, or in the case of "Dinner," minor characters, do most of the talking, permitting their auditors to make only brief remarks from time to time. In "Zone of Quiet," for example, a vain, shallow-brained nurse narrates her adventures in romance to a man patient in a hospital, each morning giving him an installment covering her activities of the night before. At best, the man manages only to interrupt with an occasional question or an attempted answer to one of hers as she babbles on and on to the conclusion of the story. In "Sun Cured," a Brooklyn insurance agent, first headed for a Florida vacation and then returning from it, insists on talking about his affairs to a man he meets on the train, never giving his listener time to make a reply or even noting what the listener attempts to say. And "Dinner" presents, not one, but two feminine monologists, talking by alternate turns to the man seated between them, without paying the least attention to his attempted replies or to his satiric jibes.

Thus, though technically third-person narratives, these three stories have the effect of first-person monologues, the main difference being that the presence of the listener is actually manifested instead of being merely implied, as in a standard monologue. Of the three, "Zone of Quiet" is by far the most skillfully done, for as the nurse daily recounts her experiences to the man in the hospital bed, the story moves forward by scenes which successively become more interesting to the patient as well as to the reader, and at the same time the interplay of the nurse's and the patient's reactions to each other furnishes an added source of interest and drama. Though Lardner utilized the same kind of dramatic interplay between the monologists and their auditors in the other two stories, neither is as successfully done as "Zone of Quiet." The scheme Lardner used in "Sun Cured" committed him not only to breaking the main character's monologue into two big installments coming a month apart in time, but also to the farfetched coincidence of having his character encounter the same listener for a second time. Using two monologists in "Dinner" necessitated Lardner's switching from one to the other without developing any story line, the purpose of the piece being to draw a satiric caricature of the two tongue-wagging bores through their meaningless talk. "Dinner" is thus good satire but hardly a short story in the usual sense of the term.

The advantages to Lardner of using such interior monologues as these, as well as shorter ones, within the framework of the third-person point of view are perhaps already obvious. He could make a character reveal himself through what he says and how he says it, as in a regular first-person narrative. But at the same time, through the remarks of the listening character, as brief as they are, he could give a running commentary on the monologue and monologist, thus providing the reader with a contrasting vantage point for viewing the talking character and consequently of arriving at the significance of the story. The interior monologue, then, permitted Lardner both to narrate and comment on the narrative while remaining the completely detached author.

Despite Lardner's skill in handling various forms of the third person, no narrative method seemed more naturally suited to his particular talent than the first person. In 1925, at the beginning of this period, he was of course already more practiced in writing in the first person than he ever became in writing in the third. But the quality which enabled him to give his first-person stories their special brilliance was his gift for language, his ability to catch the exact tone and rhythm of the speech of the type character being depicted, whether a garrulous old man as in his earlier story "The Golden Honeymoon," an ignorant small-town barber as in "Haircut," or a frivolous wife as in "Who Dealt?". Both "Haircut" and "Who Dealt?" are full-fledged monologues, the monologist in each being an uncomprehending narrator, as was the old man in "The Golden Honeymoon." The barber-narrator of "Haircut," for example, greatly admires Jim Kendall—"he certainly was a card!"—and remains totally unconscious of the fact that the story he tells throws an entirely opposite light on Kendall. The stupid wife in "Who Dealt?" unwittingly chatters out the story of her husband's disappointment in a love affair, failing to perceive that she is telling the story to the very woman and man who figured as principals in it, and thus explodes a bombshell which may wreck her marriage as well as that of the other couple. The unconsciousness of the narrators in both stories vitally contributes to the highly ironic effects produced. With no character commenting on the narrator or providing internal clues for the reader to use in judging the narrator as in the third-person stories with interior monologues, the reader himself supplies the standard by which the narrator is measured. This, however, places no burden on him, for he simply watches as Lardner has the narrators tie the rope around their necks with their own words.

By contrast to "Haircut" and "Who Dealt?", another first-person story, "Ex Parte," does place some demand on the reader's ability to discriminate, to see behind the narrator's words and judge him on terms entirely different from those on which he expects to be judged. What gives the story this quality is that the narrator is not an ignorant character babbling out a tale while his hands are engaged at another task, such as cutting hair or playing bridge. Rather, he is a college graduate of average intelligence, engaged in presenting his version of the break-up of his marriage by writing it out in a paper to be left with the executor of his estate and read after his death. Though it is doubtful that any reader would be unwary enough to accept at face value the narrator's claim that he is merely stating the facts and exaggerating nothing, the reader nevertheless is called upon to indict the narrator on more subtle grounds than the plainly and immediately obvious ones provided in "Haircut" and "Who Dealt?". These involve seeing the functional significance of the many precisely chosen details Lardner used in the story, details by means of which he made the narrator express his lack of taste, his self-pity, his self-centeredness—in short, unconsciously to draw a full-scale portrait of his self-obsession, meanness, and vulgarity. The irony in many Lardner stories breaks forth in sharp flashes, but in this one it quietly ripples through every sentence.

Besides "Haircut," "Who Dealt?", and "Ex Parte," Lardner narrated six of the other stories in some form of the first person. In "Liberty Hall," the narrator again tells the story by writing a manuscript, but the story lacks the interest and sustained irony of "Ex Parte." Two others, "I Can't Breathe" and "Now and Then" are also "written" narratives, the first told by a girl in diary form and the second by a wife in letters to a girl friend. Lardner had used both of these methods so often before that he obviously had nothing new to display in the use of either; still, in each case the narrative method is well-suited to the characters, situations, and effect: in fact, it would have been impossible for Lardner to have chosen a method better suited to expressing the ecstatic emotions of a starry-eyed teen-age girl than that of having her tell her story to her diary, so that the reader reads it looking over her shoulder. The remaining stories are ordinary examples of regular first-person stories, narrated by a main or minor character.

Lardner, then, displayed great skill and versatility in the narrative techniques he used in the stories of his peak years. Despite the freshness of his methods, however, particularly as illustrated by his handling of point of view, he employed few methods which he had not already used to some extent or which were not in wide use by other writers. Thus, in this period, he made no really new contribution to fictional technique comparable to that which he had made in the Jack Keefe stories, where he combined the epistolary technique with a startlingly original use of the vernacular idiom. What is nevertheless especially interesting about his technique during this period is that he nearly always narrated his stories from an angle which allowed him to disassociate himself from his characters. He achieved this either by writing in the third person, where he could remain almost if not entirely outside the framework of the story as the concealed or detached author, or by using a first-person narrator who obviously, not even in a remote sense, could be identified with the author, as the narrators of such stories as "Haircut," "Who Dealt?", and "I Can't Breathe" illustrate. There are, of course, some exceptions: the narrator of "Mr. and Mrs. Fix-It" is at least in part identifiable with Lardner, if we can attach any significance to what he said about the story in the spoofing preface he wrote for *The Love Nest* collection. Moreover, as already suggested, it is incorrect to say, as some of Lardner's commentators have said, that he completely obliterated himself as the omniscient author from all, or even most, of his third-person stories: not only does he sometimes speak directly around his characters to the reader, but also, in some cases, both through and around them, as "Contract" illustrates, where it is impossible to escape the conviction that Mr. Shelton, in everything but name, is really Mr. Lardner.

Despite the fact that Lardner seldom achieved complete objectivity in his third-person stories, it is notable that he never entered the minds of his characters to give an extended analysis of their psychological states, of their attitudes and thought processes. Insofar as he reveals the subjective qualities of his characters at all, he reveals them indirectly through what they say about themselves and others. The peculiar force of Lardner's narrative method is that he makes the reader see and hear and hence form his own judgment of the characters from their external rather than from their internal qualities.

The kind of narrative method Lardner used, the customary disassociation of himself from his characters, and his avoidance of subjective character analysis are closely related to the fact that he was writing satire and was resorting to narrative methods in keeping with that intention. The tenor of the satire varies in these stories, but it is consistently present, and rises to sardonic levels in such ones as "The Love Nest," "A Day with Conrad Green," "Haircut," "Dinner," and "Ex Parte." Throughout, its staple is irony: irony of statement, of situation, of a speaker unconscious of the import of his words, of the person holding a false self-image, of the juxtaposition of opposites—in short, irony of every conceivable variety. In many cases, the story titles suggest the central focus of the irony. A "love nest" is exactly the opposite of what Lou Gregg's palatial mansion is in actuality. "Liberty Hall" becomes a prison for the couple who go there to relax and secure freedom from the interference of well-wishers and business associates. The babbling nurse dispels the hospital "zone of quiet" for her patient, who intermittently reads about "vanity fair" in Thackeray's novel when not listening to the nurse demonstrate her particular brand of it. The wife who interrupts her silly chattering at the bridge table only long enough to ask "who dealt?" is herself the dealer of the real knockout hand—one dealt with words, not cards. "Travelogue" is actually a "talkalogue"; "Women" is not about women, but the other sex; and the only time the sun touches the man in "Sun Cured" is in the early morning hours as he returns from his all-night round of drinking and gambling.

Lardner might well have subtitled many of his stories

"Contrast"; for, apart from the otherwise important role that contrast played in his fiction, as it does in that of other writers, it provided for him a constant source of irony. In some cases, the irony arises simply from the contrast of opposite character types, as in "Travelogue," where a talkative girl is placed in contrast to a quiet one, or in "Dinner," where an intelligent guest is placed between two self-obsessed bores. In other cases, it arises from the contrast of opposite situations, as in "Now and Then," where a husband's behavior toward his wife shortly after marriage is juxtaposed to his opposite treatment of her three years later; or, as in "Nora," where a couple of professional libretto writers convert an author's play into a completely different one. In still other cases, the irony arises from the difference between the apparent situation and the real one, as seen in stories like "The Love Nest" and "Ex Parte."

Lardner, however, employed no form of irony more consistently and with more telling effect than that resulting from the statement of a character who is unconscious of the true significance of his words. When attempting to describe to Bartlett how marriage and motherhood have affected his wife, Lou Gregg of "The Love Nest" intends to say that they have given her poise. But that is not what he manages to say: "I mean I think she was a beautiful girl and now she's an even more beautiful woman. I mean wifehood and maternity have given her a kind of a—well, you know—I mean a kind of a pose. I mean pose" (*LN*, 14-15). And so they have, as Bartlett soon discovers, though throughout Lou Gregg remains as unconscious of the irony of what he says as do the barber in "Haircut," the wife in "Who Dealt?", the interior monologist in "Sun Cured," or the speakers in nearly any one of the stories. This was no device Lardner first began using in this period: he had used it since the first Jack Keefe story and he continued using it to the end of his career. The hallmark of the typical Lardner character is that he is unconscious that his words show him in a light entirely different from the one intended or that they convey an idea the opposite of the one he thinks he is expressing.

Naturally, both the type characters Lardner depicted and the larger elements of the methods he utilized to depict them, such as his consistent use of irony, his varied organizational schemes, and, most important, the point of view from which he wrote, dictated the style—or perhaps more correctly, styles—of the stories. In general, the most notable stylistic difference distinguishing this group of stories from his earlier ones is his more extensive employment of standard—or as he preferred to call it, "straight"—English. By writing in the third person, he could abandon the vernacular style but continue writing dialogue suited to the characters involved. In fact, Lardner very often shows a dramatic contrast between the directness and simplicity with which one character expresses himself and the twisted, ungrammatical manner in which another expresses himself. In "The Love Nest," for example, Bartlett's unadorned, correct speech is juxtaposed to Lou Gregg's tortured, pompous brand of Americanese, and similar contrasts are found in such stories as "Dinner," "Contract," and "Zone of Quiet." But in a sizable number of the third-person stories—"Anniversary," "Man Not Overboard," and "There Are Smiles," among others—as well as in some of those narrated in the first-person, the characters express themselves in fairly standard American English, though their language is colloquial and sometimes trite or even slangy. In all the stories, the characters' language reflects their educational levels, environments, and stations in life; it is the mirror of their minds, twisted or straight as they may be.

Lardner nevertheless did not altogether abandon the vernacular style in this period. The idiom of the narrator of "Mr. and Mrs. Fix-It," for example, is the same that Gullible spoke. The language of the nurse in "Zone of Quiet" closely resembles Mabelle Gillespie's in "Some Like Them Cold"—when an allowance is made, of course, for the difference between the spoken and written vernacular. And the authenticity and naturalness of the barber's vernacular speech in "Haircut" is not excelled by that used by Lardner in any other story. As these, and other examples which might be cited, indicate, Lardner had not lost his ear for the vernacular idiom; rather, he made limited use of it because he was tired of it, as he could well afford to be, after having used it so extensively throughout the first ten years of his career.

It is inevitable, however, that the quieter, more toned-down style Lardner adopted in this period must suffer by comparison with the buoyancy, the rhythmical swing, and the vivid color of his earlier one—at least, as embodied in *You Know Me Al, Gullible's Travels,* and *The Big Town.* Still, this contrast can be misleading, for if the style of this period is less spectacular, it is, on the other hand, more precisely controlled. It serves as a means to an end, never as an end in itself, as his earlier style sometimes appears to be. Though the brightly turned phrases and lively tempo of *The Big Town*'s style display the mental qualities of the character through whom Lardner narrated the work, it is apparent that the chosen narrator also permitted Lardner to display his verbal facility. By contrast, in the stories of this period, Lardner never appeared to have any stylistic objective in view other than that of writing in the manner best suited to the characters involved and to the particular tone and effect sought. Thus, the barren simplicity of the language used in "Anniversary" fits the bleak monotony of the lives led by the characters. The brighter diction and faster tempo of the sentences in "I Can't Breathe" catch the pulsating heart-beats of a teen-age girl. The strained humor and stock diction of the narrator in "Ex Parte" express the quality of his mind. The breezy jargon of the Broadway libretto writers in "Nora," the hardboiled joviality of the New York policeman in "There Are Smiles," and the meandering sentence patterns of "Who Dealt?" and "Haircut" are all in keeping with the characters presented and the effects desired.

The fact that Lardner worked with more deliberate and conscious artistry in this period than ever before does not mean that he was equally successful with all his stories or produced no poor ones. On the contrary, though he wrote most of his memorably fine short stories—his anthology pieces—in these years and achieved a high level of merit in several others, he nevertheless produced many quite mediocre ones. As already indicated, "Dinner" may be good satire, but it is not good fiction. "Now and Then" is interesting for its irony, but its structure is labored and mechanical. "There Are Smiles" and "Man Not Overboard" are typical slick magazine stories which could have been turned out by any competent *Redbook* or *Cosmopolitan* fiction writer of the day. "Old Folks' Christmas" is sentimental; "Nora" is amusing, but otherwise insignificant. Still, the percentage of good stories is high. Lardner was soon to lose creative momentum, and some of these stories show that he was already losing it; but in no other period did he display more consistent artistry than he did in this, his major one.

The Uncollected Stories

OVER HALF of the seventy-nine[1] separate short stories Lardner wrote have never appeared in book collections and consequently are available to the reader only in the pages of the magazines where they were first published. None of these stories is comparable in merit to the very best ones which have been reprinted, but at least twelve to fifteen are superior to the poorer stories appearing in *Round Up*—ones such as "Nora," "Man Not Overboard," "Reunion," "A Frame-Up," and "Old Folks' Christmas"—and many of the others are equal in quality to these. Besides the additional light the stories shed on the scope and character of Lardner's literary achievement, they also give us a fuller insight into his aims and attitudes; those written during his final years are particularly interesting for the decided change they show in the cast of his thought. Since these stories— they number thirty-nine in all—rather evenly divide themselves into an early group of eighteen published before 1922 and a later group of twenty-one appearing after 1925, this chapter considers them in that order, placing the primary emphasis on the later group.

I *The Early Group*

As might be expected, many of the eighteen earlier stories deal with sports: eight center on baseball, two on football, and one on prize fighting. All the baseball stories are narrated in the vernacular idiom from the first-person point of view of the main character or of a minor character, and they repeat the same basic structural pattern. They treat such characters as two impossibly vain pitchers who will play at their best only when placed in competition with one another;[2] an umpire of unquestionable integrity who beats up his girl friend's brother for calling him a crook;[3] a stubborn player who prefers facing starvation to taking a salary cut;[4] and another player so painfully girl-shy that he nearly faints when a girl speaks to him.[5] Despite the similarity of their structure and the frequently trivial situations they develop, the stories are expertly written; and several are witty and comic—notably, "The Poor Simp" (September, 1915), "Where Do You Get That Noise?" (October, 1915), and "The Yellow Kid" (June, 1917). Had Lardner chosen to include these stories in *How to Write Short Stories* instead of "Harmony," "Horseshoes," and "A Frame-Up" he would have improved the quality of that volume.

"The Battle of the Century" (October, 1921), the story about prize fighting, merits special attention because it is a thinly disguised fictional retelling of the Dempsey-Carpentier championship fight. Lardner's apparent purpose is to satirize the gullibility of fight fans who "like to be bunked but . . . like most of all to bunk themselves."[6] No knowledgeable fan could have regarded the small Carpentier (renamed "Goulet" in the story) as a serious challenger for Dempsey's heavyweight title. Yet, easily convincing themselves that what they wanted to believe was right and lambasting the few reporters who dared to tell them the truth, 80,000 persons paid nearly two million dollars—the fourth largest gate in boxing history—to see the handsome French war-hero knock out Dempsey but, of course, saw the reverse happen. A story so closely based on fact illustrates Lardner's ability to create satire simply by presenting an actual occurrence in story form from the viewpoint of an ironic narrator. The trenchant observations the narrator, a sportswriter, makes about human beings toward the conclusion of the story leave no room for questioning that he is Lardner's in-character mouthpiece: "Well, *I* was in New York for three days prior to the 'big fight,' and four or five days afterwards, and anybody that was there had to take a course in human nature. I didn't learn much that I hadn't suspected before, but whatever doubts I may of had was removed once and for all."[7]

Despite the fact that a majority of the earlier uncollected stories deal with sports and athletes, a sizable number—seven—focus on other types of characters and subject matter. For example, three of the seven—"Tour No. 2" (February, 1915), "The Last Night" (November, 1917), and "A Chip of the Old Block" (September, 1918)—have war backgrounds. Two others, "Tour-

Y-10" (February, 1917) and "Ball-A-Hole" (May, 1917) bear a fairly close resemblance, respectively, to "Travelogue" and "A Caddy's Diary"; for not only do they deal with the same basic character types and situations as the two collected stories, but they are of comparable merit. Still another, "A Friendly Game" (May, 1917), might well have been included in the *Gullible's Travels* sequence group, for it presents Gullible getting taken for a loss in a card game by a supposedly stupid young married couple. The remaining story "The Clubby Roadster" (February, 1918) depicts two married couples bickering their way through an automobile ride.

Perhaps the most interesting and best written story of the eighteen is "A Chip of the Old Block"—at least, it is indisputably the most satiric in the group and even ranks with such satiric masterpieces as "Champion," "The Love Nest," and "A Day with Conrad Green." Although the story refers to World War I, it could just as well refer to earlier or later wars, for the story satirizes the corps of "young warriors" produced by every war who seek the cushioned ease of rear-area appointments to escape going to the fighting front as common soldiers. The main character, Evan Barnes, whose first name means "young warrior," is the son of a man killed in the Spanish-American War and the grandson of a Civil War veteran. Going to Washington, the young warrior gets an appointment with the aid of his congressman as a captain in the "N.C.O."—non-combattant officers corps.

Naïvely recounting his experiences in letters written to his grandfather, Evan boasts: "But just think, Grandfather, here I am, only twenty-one and a captain, while you were only a sergeant at the end of the Civil War after being in it almost from the time it began."[8] Assigned to the "Sleuth" department of the "N.C.O." corps, Evan is given such dangerous duties as eavesdropping on conversations in bars and reporting suspicious characters to his headquarters, but these "duties" do not prevent his living in a plush hotel, attending dances, and wooing a girl engaged to a soldier who has been wounded in action overseas. When he and Captain Bellows, a fellow "N.C.O.," meet a distinguished general, he asks them: "Why is it some of you boys don't try to get to France?"

> Bellows said he supposed it was because most of us had been there with our parents several years ago, so it would be no novelty, and others of us preferred waiting until long enough

after the war so that the country would be rebuilt to look something like its old self. Then the General asked us if we would please get up and leave him, as he felt rather nauseated and wanted to be alone. . . . Poor old General, I suppose he is in a decline and won't be of service much longer. . . .[9]

On learning that Evan has become engaged to the wounded soldier's ex-fiancée, the grandfather writes Evan to send him the soldier's name and address and thereafter never write or visit him again. He signs the letter "Your Grandfather (God help him)."

By using the epistolary technique according to his usual method, except for writing in standard English, Lardner detached himself completely from the story; but through the grandfather and the general as well as a newspaper reporter, he established a contrasting, internal point of view for judging the young man. Thus, "A Chip of the Old Block" is an exceptionally skillfully written and powerful story. Unless it was that Lardner chose not to cast himself in the light of seeming to pound a momentarily dead issue, it is difficult to understand why he did not reprint this story in *How to Write Short Stories* or in one of his other collections.

If a few of these earlier uncollected stories are of exceptional merit and if many others are of sound quality, it follows nevertheless that they add little to one's knowledge of Lardner's early development. They show again, as Lardner's collected fiction does, that he was at first mainly preoccupied with sports and athletes. But they also indicate, again as his collected fiction does, that step by step as his career unfolded, he turned more and more to other types of characters and subject matter.

II *The Later Group*

It is an interesting coincidence that seventeen of the earlier group of uncollected stories (all but "The Battle of the Century") were produced during the first five years of Lardner's career and that a similar number of the twenty-one in the later group were produced during the last five years of it, only four appearing earlier than 1929. The two groups of stories, then, permit us to contrast the beginning and finishing stages of Lardner's career as a short story writer. The contrast is indeed a dramatic one.

According to the various attitudes Lardner displayed and the different types of characters and situations he presented, the twenty-one later stories can be arranged into three slightly overlapping groups. First, many appearing before and a few after 1930 deal with characters and situations essentially similar to those treated in the collected stories discussed in Chapter V: that is, with degraded or mean characters shown in situations where they are taking, or attempting to take, advantage of others, or otherwise violating the principles of common decency. The satiric tone of these stories is as harsh as, and sometimes even harsher than, that of such stories as "Haircut" and "The Love Nest." The second and largest group presents main characters caught in situations where they are victimized by the aggressor type presented in the first group.[10] Lardner treated these characters sympathetically, leveling his satiric fire against the minor characters who are preying upon the focal ones. Finally, the third and smallest group presents characters who are not victims of their fellow man so much as of fate—fate in the form of an illness or of a chronic habit which they cannot overcome. These characters are treated compassionately, and the satire present is based on tragic irony. Though Lardner made little display of his own ailments in his writing, some of the stories in this group suggest that in his final years his thoughts were preoccupied with illness.

The first group is best illustrated by "The Jade Necklace" (November, 1926), "The Venomous Viper of the Volga" (September, 1927), "Stop Me—If You've Heard This One" (July, 1929), "Pity Is Akin" (September, 1929), "That Old Sweetheart of Mine" (November, 1929), and "Greek Tragedy" (February, 1935). Without exception, these are poor stories, none being comparable in merit to the poorest ones in *Round Up*. Despite their artistic inferiority, however, they do give us further insight into Lardner's concern with human vanity, brutality, and coarseness.

"The Jade Necklace" treats a theme Lardner also developed in "Nora" and to some extent in several other stories, that of the show producer who purchases an original work and then hires professional libretto writers to mutilate it beyond recognition, or, as in this story, convert it into a pale copy of another show. By contrast, "The Venomous Viper of the Volga" and "Greek Tragedy" satirize the professional sports of boxing and wrestling; but both stories ridicule not only the athletes but also their fans and crooked promoters. The "Venomous Viper" is a huge ex-Pennsylvania coal miner whom a fight promoter and a clever press agent attempt to publicize as a famous "foreign" boxer in order to match him with the champion and thus draw a big gate, though the champion will surely win the fight. In the process, they have vulgar pictures tatooed on his chest to give him more appeal to "Fistic Fandom, or Moronia," and in a framed-up bout they pit him against a consumptive ex-fighter, whom the Viper kills with a blow. The novice boxer's career ends abruptly, however, when he is soundly thrashed by the undersized press agent whose girl friend's affections the Viper has alienated. Vainly, the Viper tries to prevent the beating by telling the press agent that "She's been my girl pretty near ever since I bashed the poor Espagnola. It was them tatto pictures that made her love me."[11] In "Greek Tragedy," clever publicity has billed a wrestling match between Greek Alexis and Big Bill Buell into a "grudge" fight, and the story presents them in the ring apparently engaging in a vicious battle before a large audience. But actually the two are good friends; as they take falls by prearranged turns, they are carrying on a quiet and friendly conversation, the topic of which centers on the alarming news that a man from the Greek's hometown, where the Greek is wanted by the sheriff, has become a sports writer and may recognize the Greek. When they see the man come in, the Greek pretends to sprain his ankle so that the match is stopped, and the Greek flees.

Obviously, the situations of both stories are farfetched, the characters are crudely despicable as any Lardner ever presented, and the satire, in keeping with the nature of the subject matter, is coarse-grained. Lardner had never really admired prize fighting or fighters, and he apparently held an equally low opinion of wrestling. But in these stories, as in his earlier "The Battle of the Century," Lardner directed harsh criticism against the public followers of such barbaric sports, seeing the willingness of fans to be bunked and bilked as the primary motivation behind crooked fight promotion. Though both stories are written in the third person, Lardner intrudes in one to tell the reader that the Viper bore "a striking resemblance to a fight crowd's common grandpa, the ape,"[12] and in the other to say that "the average wrestling fan . . . was not sure whether Greece was a suburb of Berlin or an Asiatic monarchy. . . ."[13] By such statements as these, as well as by the characters and events used in the stories,

Lardner made his thorough objection to these sports plainly evident.

Though the other three stories belonging to this group are equally satiric, they are painfullly thin and contrived. "Stop Me— If You've Heard This One" is a take off on a famous raconteur who converts the stories he hears other people tell into his own, retelling them as though they had happened to him. "That Old Sweetheart of Mine" shows a wife and her former boyfriend fatuously attempting to warm up their old romance, though neither is really any longer interested in the other. "Pity Is Akin" is the melodramatic story of a prohibition agent who brings a featured night-club singer to trial for being part owner of a club where drinks are sold, sees her acquitted by the jury even when she is reeking with whiskey, and then falls in love with her. But no romance blossoms because the angry singer gets a husky head-waiter to punch the would-be lover in the jaw and evict him from her place of business. This story is a fictionalized presentation of two pet grievances which Lardner touched on more frequently in his nonfiction than in his fiction: the tendency of a jury to acquit a woman regardless of the evidence indicting her, and the sheer folly of attempting to enforce a law to which the general public objects, as was the case with the Volstead Act. But despite the further insights these stories afford into Lardner's critical attitudes and of the defects he found in American society, they show his artistry as a fiction writer at the level of mere hackwork.

By contrast to the mean, vulgar, or insipid main characters appearing in the first group of stories, those in the second are decent persons caught in situations, sometimes partly of their own making, where they are misunderstood, mistreated, or even ruined by others. Victimized main characters had appeared in such earlier Lardner stories as "Anniversary," "Now and Then," and "The Maysville Minstrel." Moreover, the dumb boobs Lardner depicted during the first decade of his career were often victims also, though they were victimized by their own ignorance and stupidity and not by other characters. Although Lardner had treated these characters sympathetically, he nevertheless satirized them, as in a sense he also satirized the main characters of "Anniversary," "Now and Then," and "The Maysville Minstrel." But his attitude toward the victimized main characters in his late stories is wholly sympathetic, the satire being directed entirely at the minor characters responsible for bringing harm to the major ones.

"Great Blessings" (December, 1929) and "Bob's Birthday" (November, 1933) serve as convenient introductory illustrations to the stories in this group, for they show not only the sympathetic manner with which Lardner treated the characters, but also the grim situations he placed them in. "Great Blessings," a "Thanksgiving" story, opens with the president's Thanksgiving proclamation, which says in part: "Our fields have been abundantly productive, our industries have flourished, our commerce has increased, wages have been lucrative, and comfort and contentment have followed the undisturbed pursuit of honest toil."[14] Against this cheerful official assurance that all is well and that throughout the land happy, loving family clans are gathering at tables heaped with the abundance of the season, Lardner projects a grim, melancholy story. Clara Stewart has turned down an earnest, hard-working man to marry a handsomer one who proves to be a worthless rotter; the upshot is that Clara now lives in a poverty-stricken household. What compounds her misery, however, is that her husband's obnoxious parents come for frequent visits, on the Thanksgiving featured in the story as well as other times. They come not only to gobble up the food Clara manages to place on the table, but also to give her advice on rearing her child, advice which they are least qualified to give. For one of their two sons is a bootlegger, and the other—Clara's husband—is a lazy incompetent, unable to hold a job and, moreover, a philanderer carrying on an affair with a woman of bad reputation. The parents themselves are poor managers of their own lives, being in debt to their landlord because they throw away money on trifling luxuries. Thus, married to a worthless man, living in poverty, and encroached upon by nagging, predatory in-laws, the main character of this story enjoys no "great blessings" but suffers great misery, which she hardly deserves despite her wrong choice of a husband.

Narrated by the fourteen-year-old sister of the main character, his one family sympathizer, "Bob's Birthday" is an equally grim story about a seventeen-year-old boy who supports his sister, his father, his mother, and an uncle and aunt by playing in an orchestra. His father and uncle are out of work and with their spouses spend their time drinking and going to parties, "borrowing" their gin money and taxi fare from Bob and eating the food he provides. On Bob's birthday, they come in from an all-night party and bring his grandfather—now also unemployed and so drunk he can say nothing more than "Hotcha"—to him as a "present." The climax to Bob's "happy birthday" comes, however, when his girl friend and her father pay a surprise call on the disheveled, noisy family; Bob's father tells the girl's father that he will not allow Bob to marry his daughter, "not if she was the last girl in the world." Thus, with this romance spoiled, Bob has himself, his sister, and five worthless, ungrateful adults to support.

Some of the stories in this group are less melodramatic than these two; the misery is not heaped quite so high on their main characters as upon Clara and Bob, though they all suffer in one way or another. "Freedom of the Press" (November, 1935), for example, presents a wealthy girl who is victimized by the press, reporters invading her privacy at every turn, one even showing up at the door of her private compartment when she goes on her honeymoon. "Poodle" (January, 1934), one of the best stories Lardner wrote in his final years, depicts a man victimized both by the Depression, which throws him out of work, and by his nagging, termagant wife, who abuses him and thinks he is consorting with other women. Unknown to the wife, the man has found another job, that of being the caretaker of a wealthy mental patient, who calls him "Poodle." At the end, the character bitterly summarizes his position as follows: "I'm a seventy-two hundred dollar day nurse named Poodle. I spend eight hours a day with a crazy person that pays and the rest of the time with one that doesn't."[15] In "Take a Walk" (October, 1933), a baseball umpire is wrongly accused of hitting a player, and the ensuing complications result in his losing his fiancée, quitting his umpiring job, and going to live with a relative in Texas. Finally, a few of the stories in this group—such as "The Spinning Wheel" (July, 1927), "High Rollers" (June, 1929), and "Words and Music" (August, 1930)—present main characters who discover with horror that they have been duped by people they admire; they are victims only in the sense that they suffer painful initiations into the meanness, falsity, and hypocrisy of their fellow man.

The third and final category of Lardner's late stories is best represented by "Mamma" (June, 1930), "Cured!" (March, 1931), and "Widow" (October, 1935). Of these, "Mamma," based on a real-life story that Lardner's wife heard when she was doing voluntary social work (Elder, 320), is the grimmest and most melancholy. It is the story of a woman who, when picked up and quizzed by the police in Grand Central Station, can only reply that her name is "Mamma." She is taken to a hospital and under the prompting of a doctor and nurse, she finally recalls that her last name is Carns. When the nurse tracks down her address, she discovers that the woman's husband and two children have recently died of flu. The doctor and nurse thereupon decide not to try to make "Mamma" recall the whole story: they reason that she is in a more blessed state out of her mind than she would be in if she regained it. The sheer horror and morbidity of "Mamma," as well as its surprise ending, suggest a typical Ambrose Bierce story.

Neither main character of the other two stories is so wholly a victim of fate as is "Mamma." "Cured!," which may reflect the struggle Lardner waged with drink, deals with a cartoonist who has become a chronic alcoholic and is unable to rid himself of the habit even with the aid of a doctor. In "Widow," a woman suddenly loses her husband when he is stricken with a heart attack; and the maudlin friends, who pour in to see her weep, wonder why she is dry-eyed. The reason is that she has not really loved her husband and is secretly glad that she is now free to marry a man she does love. But in the retrospect his death brings, her husband suddenly looms up as a very honorable man, now greatly admired by the very pals who joked about him when he was alive. Caught in this revulsion of feeling, the man she loves comes to tell her that he can have nothing further to do with her because of his respect for her dead husband—a cruel twist of fate, for the man has felt perfectly free to lead her on by flirting with her when her husband was living.

Finally, one other story, fitting none of the categories into which the other uncollected stories group themselves, is interesting, not because it has literary merit, but because it shows how painfully difficult fiction writing became for Lardner after 1930. Entitled "Insomnia" (May, 1931) and plainly autobiographical, the story presents a story writer lying in bed unable to sleep, his mind working on and on in an effort to conjure up plots for stories. He wishes he were "as good as O. Henry and could get by with a thousand or twelve hundred word," for then, he tells himself, "I could write a thousand-word short story every day; that is, I could if my head were as full of plots as his must have been."[16] As his thoughts run on, he recalls a boyhood romance which has been broken up by the girl's parents and then remembers a longer story about a man who kills himself by going on a wild drinking spree. But the emphasis falls not on the interior stories, which are merely summarized, but upon the sleepless writer and his weary efforts to think of an idea he can convert into a saleable story.

The direct evidence this story provides—that Lardner in his final years, working under the painful disadvantage of his growing illness, continued writing fiction only with great difficulty—is corroborated as well by the inferior quality of the other stories. Particularly those published after 1929 show that his abilities were steadily deteriorating, for they are forced and mechanical in technique, their situations contrived and farfetched, and their tone dreary and spiritless. To be sure, there are a number of exceptions, after 1930 as well as before: "High Rollers," "The Spinning Wheel," and "Poodle" are stories of good quality, and the technique of some—that of "Mamma" and "Words and Music," for example—is quite deft. Further, it should be remembered that *Lose with a Smile* (see Chapter II) belongs to this period and is the most sustained and creditable fictional effort Lardner made in his final years, even though it is inferior to his earlier busher stories.

Such works as *Lose with a Smile* and "Mamma," however, suggest another change which occurred in the character of Lardner's fiction after 1929: the shift to grim, melancholy, or even morbid subject matter. Though the atmosphere of such earlier stories as "Champion," "Haircut," or "The Love Nest" is hardly to be described as pleasant, that which lingers over many of his late ones is one of death, illness, or intense human misery. In his use of victimized and suffering main characters of the kind appearing in groups two and three above, Lardner showed a marked change in attitude in his later fiction. By treating these characters sympathetically and compassionately, he appeared to identify his misery with theirs; and, whether it resulted from his own illness or from the change of his pessimism into despair, a note of resignation, of hopelessness and helplessness, is unmistakably evident in many of these stories. To the end, Lardner continued to employ irony and satire, but his last stories show that he had pretty clearly given up such hope as he may once have had that dignity, honesty, and fairness would ever prevail in the tangled web of human affairs.

CHAPTER 7

Lardner's Nonfiction

IN THE COURSE of a career which included serving as a reporter for eight years, as a daily columnist for another six, and as a weekly columnist for over seven years, Lardner did a vast amount of newspaper writing. He also contributed more than a hundred pieces to magazines, wrote a number of special essays for books, conducted a radio column in *The New Yorker* for one and a half years, and collaborated with George S. Kaufman in writing a three-act play. Besides sports reporting, columns, radio reviews, and drama, he wrote comic essays and sketches, parodies, burlesque biographies, nonsense playlets, and verse. Little wonder that Lardner always described himself as a journalist. For, despite the fact that his literary fame rests on his fiction, he was a journalist from the beginning to the end of his career, steadily engaged in discharging regular commitments to newspapers and doing free-lance writing on his own as his time and inclination permitted.

Although Lardner probably realized that most of this work was ephemeral, during his lifetime he published seven book collections of nonfiction besides *Regular Fellows I Have Met* (1919) and the play *June Moon* (1930); and at his death, he had in progress still an eighth collection, which Gilbert Seldes subsequently completed. These volumes shed no direct light on Lardner's fiction; but besides the interest they command in their own right, they contribute to a fuller understanding of Lardner's literary achievement and are thus worthy of brief examination.

I *Verse*

Chronologically, *Bib Ballads* (1915) is not only Lardner's first collection of nonfiction but also the first volume of creative work he published.[1] To escape the deadly routine of writing a regular column seven days a week, it was his custom to compose a few verses for his Monday Chicago *Tribune* column, "In the Wake of the News," and *Bib Ballads* is a collection of thirty of these poems. As the title suggests, they deal with children—in fact, with Lardner's own children, for he was just then becoming accustomed to fatherhood. The poems are, as Elder noted, "tender and unabashedly sentimental" (97); and perhaps for this precise reason, they became a popular feature of the "Wake" column.[2] This is a typical one:

His Favorite Role

You could be president as well as not,
    Since all you'd have to do is think you were.
With that imagination that you've got:
    Or multimillionaire if you prefer,
Or you could be some famous football star.
    Or Tyrus Cobb, admired by ev'ry fan:
Instead of that, you tell me that you are
    The Garbage Man.

Why pick him out, when you can take your choice?
    Is his so charming, nice, and sweet a role
That acting it should make you to rejoice
    And be a source of comfort to your soul?
Is there some hidden happiness that he
    Uncovers in his march from can to can
That you above all else should want to be
    The Garbage Man?

Fortunately, Lardner did not specialize in this tender variety of verse but rather in the comic, spoofing type seen in *Regular Fellows I Have Met*, as well as in some of his magazine pieces and even in a few of his short stories. Doubtless, Lardner's lifelong fondness for versifying went along with his interest in song-writing and music, but he laid no claim to poetic ability and composed verse more for his own amusement than for any other reason.

II *Humor and Satire*

Lardner's next volume of nonfiction, *My Four Weeks in France* (1918), consisted of eight articles he produced on assignment as a war reporter for *Collier's* and first published in that magazine under the title, *Reporter's Diary*. In carrying out the assignment, Lardner was unable to make the journey to France on a troop ship as he had desired; he never got closer than one and a half miles to the front lines; and he talked with only a few American officers and men. The articles thus are not about war but about the people he met on the trip, the little adventures which befell him, the peculiarities of the French language, the zaniness of Paris taxicab drivers, and other features of French life and customs which American journalists visiting Paris over the years have exploited as standard topics for humor. But even if the subject matter lacks originality, the articles are entertaining reading—particularly the one forming Chapter VI, where Lardner described the ridiculously comic struggle he had with French bureaucracy and red tape as he sought to do a simple favor for an American major. In the other chapters, as in this one, Lardner created the humor by exaggerating and dramatizing his own experiences and by giving comic portrayals of the people he encountered; but at times a serious undertone showed through the humor as he touched on things suggesting the nearness and the reality of the war, such as the crippled soldiers on the streets, the appalling number of women dressed in black, and Americans engaged in dead-earnest battle training. Further, Lardner ridiculed various types of war hangers-on, such as idle sight-seeing tourists and sensation seekers, none provoking him to more scorn than those who falsely claimed a firsthand experience with the fighting front or who otherwise laid claim to a knowledge they did not have. In his nonfiction as well as in his fiction, Lardner recorded his intense dislike of pretension, falsehood, and hyprocrisy. But despite occasional vivid passages, both serious and comic, *My Four Weeks in France* is a thin work which added nothing to Lardner's stature as a writer.

In fairly rapid succession, Lardner next published three small volumes, each containing a single humorous essay which had seen prior publication in a magazine. These are *The Young Immigrunts* (1920), *Symptoms of Being 35* (1921), and *Say It with Oil* (1923). Written at a magazine editor's request as a reply to a synthetic attack Nina Wilcox Putnam had made on husbands in an essay (also printed between the same covers), *Say It with Oil* is decidedly the poorest of the three. The contrived quality of its humor prompted Robert Benchley to describe the piece as "a typical magazine editor's idea, and the fact that Mr. Lardner got some laughs into it doesn't make it any better. There are plenty of things that Ring Lardner ought to be doing, without spending his time trying to rewrite something that editors have been suggesting to funny men for hundreds of years."³

The subject of *Symptoms of Being 35*, that of the changes in viewpoints and habits which occur as one grows older, is equally time-worn. But the humor of the work is brighter and more spontaneous, illustrating at its best Lardner's characteristic blending of the vernacular idiom with such standby humor devices as word play, anticlimax, exaggeration, malapropisms, and ludicrous figures of speech. The position Lardner took in the essay on his growing older was that he was "makeing no complaints to the management."

The Young Immigrunts is the best of the three and one of the finest pieces of humor Lardner created. Using as the central topic the motor trip which he, his wife, and one son made in the fall of 1919 from Goshen, Indiana, to Greenwich, Connecticut, Lardner wrote *The Young Immigrunts* in a style parodying that of *The Young Visiters*, a recent work allegedly written by twelve-year-old Daisy Ashford and published with an introduction by Sir James Barrie, who claimed to have made few changes in the manuscript. Lardner imitated its "lordly" prose, misspellings, and simplified sentence structure and presented *The Young Immigrunts* as though it had been written by his four-year-old son, Ring Junior. The following passage illustrates the flavor and quality of the humor. The Lardners are making the boat crossing from Detroit to Buffalo and observe a newly married couple:

> A little latter who should come out on the porch and set them-selfs ner us but the bride and glum.
>
> Oh I said to myself I hope they will talk so as I can hear them as I have always wandered what newlyweds talk about on their way to Niagara Falls and soon my wishs was realized.
>
> Some night said the young glum are you warm enough.
>
> I am perfectly comfertible replid the fare bride tho her looks belid her words what time do we arive in Buffalo.
>
> 9 oclock said the lordly glum are you warm enough.
>
> I am perfectly comfertible replid the fare bride what time do we arive in Buffalo.
>
> 9 oclock said the lordly glum I am afrade it is too cold for you out here.

Well maybe it is replid the fare bride and without farther adieu they went in the spacius parlers.

I wander will he be arsking her 8 years from now is she warm enough said my mother with a faint grimace.

The weather may change before then replid my father.

Are you warm enough said my father after a slite pause.

No was my mothers catchy reply.[4]

The Young Immigrunts displays the special flair Lardner had for parody, a type of writing seemingly well suited to his humorous and satiric bent.

Lardner quite accurately described the contents of his next nonfiction collection, *What of It?* (1925), by saying in the preface that the work in the volume was "miscellaneous magazine and newspaper stuff, on all kinds of subjects." The first of its four divisions, "The Other Side," is the rather lengthy account of a trip Lardner and his wife made to France, where they visited the Fitzgeralds on the Riviera and then toured such places as Paris, London, and Glasgow. The second division is composed of three nonsense plays; the third, of four "Bed-Time Stories" (actually burlesque fairy stories); and the fourth, "Obiter Dicta," of some two dozen satiric, comic, or nonsense sketches.

In two of the most interesting of the last group, "In Conference" and "Business is Business," Lardner satirized the stereotyped idea stated in the title of the second, an idea central to the American businessman's philosophy—namely, that "business is business." The first presents the board members of a business firm, a company of "efficiency engineers," wrestling in a lengthy conference with the grave problem of what to do about a postage-due letter which is being held for the firm at the main post office. Meanwhile, since such a business conference is sacred and not to be interrupted under any circumstances, one board member remains ignorant of the fact that his wife is leaving town with another man. "Business is Business" presents an equally ludicrous situation, but the satire is more stinging: a fire company whose membership is composed of volunteer local trades and professional people goes to a rich man's house to put out a minor blaze, and the firemen literally wreck the man's house in order to share the business involved in repairing it.

Besides these two pieces, several other good satiric sketches are in the volume. "A Close-Up of Domba Splew," for example, takes off a famous poet who has worked all winter on these verses:

> Quiescent, a person sits heart and soul,
> Thinking of daytime and Amy Lowell.
> A couple came walking along the street;
> Neither of them had ever met (92-93).

"What of It?," which gives the volume its title, shows a man giving a chronic pullman-car talker his comeuppance by replying to his every remark with "what of it?" And in "Why Authors?" Lardner derided show producers who permitted actors to revise freely and thus ruin the lines written for them by professional writers. But along with the better pieces are many very poor ones, and even a few, such as "Who's It?" and "Tennis by Cable," which are downright silly, the humor simply failing to come off.

III *Nonsense Plays and Autobiography*

To pass over *The Story of a Wonder Man* (1927) for the moment, Lardner, in his final collection of nonfiction, *First and Last*, aimed "to select from his early and later writings, those pieces which were not entirely transient and to group them in such a way as to give them . . . cohesion."[5] But they possess no more cohesion than those of *What of It?*, and the types of writing included are the same: satiric sketches, parodies, and similar pieces, some being reprinted from earlier collections. What is perhaps most noteworthy is that the volume contains nine of Lardner's short plays; two of these, "Thompson's Vacation" and "The Bull Pen," are comedy skits, but the other seven are nonsense plays, which represent one of the most interesting phases of Lardner's minor work.

The nonsense plays have evoked enthusiastic critical applause, but there is no common agreement regarding their import or significance. With their irrationality, strange characters, senseless dialogue, and meaningless action, they have been variously interpreted as a dramatization of the disorder and confusion of the modern world, as the prose equivalent of French "dada" painting, as a burlesque of expressionistic drama, and as a commentary on the breakdown of communication in the modern world. Though the plays lend at least some justification to any one of these viewpoints, Donald Elder has perhaps adopted the soundest position of all by holding that they are "a commentary on nothing except the absurdity of everything" (288).

The plays are weird conglomerations of commonplace fact and highly imaginative fantasy, of absurdity and reasonableness, of the rational and irrational. Acts are left out or combined because "nothing seemed to happen" in them, or one act is substituted for another. The action takes place in settings as inconceivable as "The Outskirts of a Parchesi Board," "A One-Street in Jeopardy," "A Public Street in a Bathroom," and "A Poultry Yard at a Spa." The casts of characters include such notable persons as "Walter Winchell, a Nun," "Theodore Dreiser, a Former Follies Girl," "H. L. Mencken, a Kleagle in the Moose," and "Casey Jones, a Midwife"; but the characters who appear may be ones entirely different from those listed in the cast, often being creatures as strange as queels, bearded glue lifters, snail gunders, and zebus.

As these jumbled, disparate characteristics suggest, the humor of the plays originates primarily from different types of incongruity. One type is that resulting from the mixture of identifiable and well-known personalities with the strange ones of Lardner's own invention. A second is that arising from the disparity between the characters and the action in which they are engaged. In "Cora, or Fun at a Spa," for example, two milch cows are presented sitting at a table playing draughts; in "Taxidea Americana," Senator La Follette is shown practicing sliding to base; and, in "Dinner Bridge," a character mimics public buildings. Still a third type of incongruity is that resulting from the use of *non sequiturs* in the dialogue, as in this passage from "I Gaspiri":

FIRST STRANGER

Where was you born?

SECOND STRANGER

Out of wedlock.

FIRST STRANGER

That's a mighty pretty country around there.

(*First and Last*, 371-72)

And the following is a second example from "Taxidea Americana":

[138]

PAT

I certainly feel sorry for people on the ocean to-night.

MIKE

What makes you think so?

(*First and Last,* 375)

Lardner, however, used no language device more consistently or with more apparent relish than he did the play on words, as Act 2 of "Abend Di Anni Nouveau" will illustrate:

ACT 2

(The interior of an ambulance. Three men named Louie Breese are playing bridge with an interne. The interne is Louie Breese's partner. Louie leads a club. The interne trumps it.)

BREESE: Kindly play interne.

INTERNE: I get you men confused.

BREESE: I'm not confused.

THE OTHER TWO BREESES: Neither of us is confused.

(They throw the interne onto Seventh Avenue. An East Side gangster, who was being used as a card table, gets up and stretches.)

GANGSTER: Where are we at?

BREESE: Was you the stretcher we was playing on?

GANGSTER: Yes.

BREESE: There's only three of us now. Will you make a fourt'?

GANGSTER: There's no snow.

(*First and Last,* 364-65)

Though these plays represent at its best the strong penchant Lardner displayed throughout his career for humor based on absurdity, they constitute only a small fraction of the nonsense writing he published. At a rough estimate no less than half of his magazine contributions was composed of nonsense, and from the time he began the *Tribune* "In the Wake of the News" column in 1913 to the time he stopped writing for the Bell Syndicate in 1927, he filled his newspaper columns with nonsense.[6] In fact, the last Bell columns he wrote were devoted to installments of his burlesque autobiography, which soon appeared in book form as *The Story of a Wonder Man* (1927).

Lardner wrote this work as a take off on the "success story" autobiography of the type represented by Edward Bok's *The*

Americanization of Edward Bok and further, to judge from the references he made to "Henry 'Peaches' Adams," he must also have had in mind *The Education of Henry Adams*. But even though *The Story of a Wonder Man* has a more clearly defined satiric aim than is apparent in the plays, it is also, as the plays are, "a picnic on the summit of absurdity."[7] The progressive adventures of the "wonder man" bear little similarity to the events of Lardner's own life. They include such wild ones as his serving as a squirrel tender in a Seattle park, his duties being to keep the squirrels out of the trees so that the people can sit in them; going to Yale and captaining the football team in his freshman year; being introduced into high society and meeting a girl whose father has bought her three tigers in the hope of breaking her of the habit of saying "Sis-boom-ah! Tiger!"; becoming a star reporter on the tabloid *The Rabies;* and marrying and divorcing a 212-pound blonde charmer, "Hugga Much." These successive occurrences permitted Lardner not only to ridicule his own success story and the type in general, but also to introduce much incidental satire on other topics—college athletics, tabloid newspapers, high society, and divorce trials.

This same kind of absurdity characterizes nine uncollected biographical sketches of famous persons which Lardner wrote for *Collier's* magazine in 1928 and 1929. His subjects included such notable personalities as David Belasco, John Barrymore, Will Rogers, and Babe Ruth. Though these sketches burlesque the achievements of their subjects as Lardner burlesqued his own success in *The Story of a Wonder Man,* they are more comic than satiric in aim, the humor being created by the simple device of presenting nationally known persons in a ridiculous light.

IV *June Moon*

Finally, the remaining volume of Lardner's nonfiction is composed of the play *June Moon,* which represents the one success he achieved in his long and determined effort to write for the stage, and he achieved this one only because he had the expert collaboration of George S. Kaufman. Adapted from Lardner's short story "Some Like Them Cold," the play uses the same two main characters (renamed Fred Stevens and Edna Baker) and the same basic plot situation, that of a young man's going to New York to embark on a career as a popular song writer. The play nevertheless bears little similarity to the short story, for its satire is directed at Broadway song writers rather than at a couple engaging in a fatuous flirtation; and the main struggle centers on the efforts of the song writer to free himself from the clutches of a predatory gold digger, the discarded mistress of a song publisher. In the end, with the aid of a kind piano player and of Paul Sears, his song-writing teammate, Fred Stevens wins out and is reunited with Edna, who has been hopefully waiting in the wings for him. The dialogue of the play is spritely and witty, the characters are plausible and real, and the situations are handled adroitly. Thus *June Moon* is a competent piece of work, but it can hardly be regarded as greatly superior to the many run-of-the-mill plays that are annually produced in the Broadway theater.

Lardner's nonfiction, then, taken together with his fiction, shows that he was a versatile writer who turned his hand to nearly every conceivable type of literature, though with unequal success, as might be expected when much of it was produced to fulfill specific assignments. Viewed as a whole, what is particularly striking about the nonfiction is not its miscellaneous or varying quality, but rather that a substantial quantity of it is sheer comic nonsense and some of it wild absurdity. Whether or not one likes the nonsense plays, the burlesque biographies, the parodies, and the numerous similar pieces Lardner wrote will depend somewhat on the brand of humor one likes—on whether one has a taste for imaginative absurdity or prefers the more earth-bound variety of humor that is based on recognizable characters and real-life situations, as in Lardner's short stories. The comparison of the mood, tone, and substance of most of Lardner's miscellaneous work with those of his short stories enables one to see clearly why he held a dual reputation in his day as a comic and serious writer.

CHAPTER 8

Lardner's Reputation and Literary Position

WITH characteristic dogmatism H. L. Mencken prophesied in 1924 that Ring Lardner was doomed to be neglected by "the professors of his own day . . . who would no more venture to whoop him up publicly and officially than their predecessors of 1880 would have ventured to whoop up Mark Twain. . . ." But after this contemporary neglect, Mencken insisted, a later generation of professors would discover Lardner and serve him up "as a sandwich between introduction and notes" in the same manner that a professor had just served up T. C. Haliburton, the creator of "Sam Slick." In the meantime, with the progressive development of American civilization, the dialect Lardner used and the "low down Americans" he depicted would have passed into limbo so that, ironically, his fiction would have lost its meaning and interest.[1]

The question of whether or not the very qualities on which the merit of Lardner's fiction rests—his authentic rendering of the common American speech and the distinctively American character types of his day—will in time cause it to become dated is an important one. But this issue, as well as others which bear upon Lardner's present and future literary standing, can be more conveniently treated in the context of the critical reputation Lardner has so far earned than at this point. Thus, this chapter first surveys Lardner's reputation and then takes up the question of his literary importance.

I *Reputation*

Mencken was dead wrong in predicting that academic critics would neglect Lardner until long after his death, for two of the best early appraisals of his work were made by professors;[2]

moreover the record shows that Lardner's work was not neglected during his lifetime either by academic or non-academic critics, nor has it since been neglected. To the contrary, for a writer who is reputed to have "blushed to the ears when hailed as a literary artist,"[3] Lardner received a great amount of critical attention in his own day, nearly all of it highly favorable; and by now a very substantial volume of commentary exists on him and his works. It is perhaps not surprising that this commentary contains distortions and inaccuracies; but regardless of these, much of the commentary is valid, a fact which shows that Lardner's works have been generally well understood and widely appreciated.

The one type of neglect Lardner did suffer, but only briefly, was that his reputation initially lagged somewhat behind his accomplishments. He had produced much highly creditable work before the mid-1920's; yet widespread recognition came only after he published *How to Write Short Stories* and *The Love Nest*. As sudden and magical as his jump from the pages of the *Saturday Evening Post* into the serious literary world appeared to be, it was not totally unheralded, for a few critics and at least one fellow short story writer had already perceived that he was no mere magazine writer and popular humorist. In early 1922, John V. Weaver, for example, suggested that it was erroneous to continue to view Lardner only as a humorist; he was ". . . in point of fact, a serious artist, a realist of the front rank. . . ."[4] In the same year, Sherwood Anderson expressed his opinion: "There is often, in a paragraph of [Lardner's], more understanding of life, more human sympathy, more salty wisdom than in hundreds of pages of, say, Mr. Sinclair Lewis's dreary prose. . . ."[5]

And as might be assumed, Mencken himself was an early Lardner champion, though it was Lardner's accurate rendering of the vernacular idiom rather than the other qualities of his work which first caught Mencken's attention. He credited Lardner with being the first writer to reduce to print common American speech, noting that he reported it "not only with humor, but also with the utmost accuracy."[6] Carl Van Doren, who in 1923 made one of the most balanced early appraisals of Lardner's work, also laid stress on the authenticity of his dialect but found his work lacked variety "in all but language." He contended that Lardner had created only two characters: first, Jack Keefe, "bragging about his prowess in love and war . . ."; and, second, "a case-hardened low-brow, under whatever name, seeing the world with his slightly snobbish wife."[7] Though in regarding Gullible, Gross, and Finch as a single character type Van Doren overlooked important differences which distinguish them from one another, his appraisal was nevertheless a reasonably just one, fairly in keeping with the fiction collections Lardner had published to that date.

Thus, a serious reputation was already in the making for Lardner before the mid-1920's, but this scattered early praise was nothing compared to the resounding burst of acclaim he received from 1924 to and following his death in 1933. Critics, important and unimportant ones alike, seemed to vie with one another in the glowing epithets they used to describe his fiction. Edmund Wilson, for example, said that "Ring Lardner seems to have imitated nobody, and nobody else could reproduce his essence."[8] Robert Littell, as was true of nearly all other critics, emphasized Lardner's ability to reproduce common American speech, saying that "Lardner lives [the] American idiom and talks it, which is one reason why the talk of his baseball heroes and their girls is so much truer to life than the 'realistic' lingo Mr. Sinclair Lewis imputes to his characters."[9] Donald Douglas thought Lardner had examined American life "with a more luminous intelligence than perhaps any other writer of these times" and that his stories wore "the magical garment of [a] prose now cleaned of all its impurities and shining like a web in the sun."[10] Mencken returned to the charge again, saying in a 1926 review of *The Love Nest* that he commended "this volume to those critics who have fallen into the habit of treating Mr. Lardner as a mere harmless clown, comparable to Kin Hubbard and Bugs Baer." Continuing, he said that readers would find in the book "satire of the most acid and appalling sort—satire wholly removed, like Swift's before it, from the least weakness of amiability, or even pity."[11] Struck by the fact that "critics of some discretion were . . . placing Lardner in the front rank of American short-story writers," Stuart Sherman "made haste to acquire and read . . . his books"; the result was that Sherman concluded that Lardner was "the hardest and leanest of contemporary wits . . . a sardonic satirist with a grip on his characters cruelly hard."[12]

It nevertheless should not be inferred from such glowing

tributes as these and others which might be cited that there was no critical dissent about the merit of Lardner's work or even that the critics who praised it most highly found no limitations or defects in it. A reviewer of *How to Write Short Stories* praised it as "one hundred per cent American" but objected strongly to its language, the very quality that most critics were applauding.[13] While finding Lardner's characters and dialogue natural and alive, another critic found the mechanics of his stories "artificially farcical,"[14] as indeed some are; for Lardner was never so much concerned with neatly-tailored plots as he was with his characters. Still another critic, in reviewing *Round Up*, objected that Lardner lacked the ability to "identify himself with his characters, to present their strongest emotions, to show how even the moron has his relations with heaven and hell, to touch on the deeper chords of life, love, and death."[15]

It was not Lardner's objective method, however, that concerned Edmund Wilson, but rather the question of whether Lardner could break away from the popular journalism to which he seemed committed, acknowledge to himself that he was a serious artist, and "go on to his *Huckleberry Finn*."[16] Lardner's apparent failure to take his work seriously and his steady derision of the idea that he was a serious artist troubled others—notably, F. Scott Fitzgerald, who thought that Lardner was wasting on relatively trivial writing a great talent which deserved to be utilized in creating a big work.[17] But others took Lardner's indifference to laying claim to a serious literary standing merely as an indication that "he had too many high-priced magazine fish to fry to worry about his place in the pantheon of American literature."[18] Yet, despite the reservations some critics expressed about his work and the disturbance which he stirred up in others by his seemingly blithe indifference to what he had achieved or what he might achieve, the chorus of acclaim rolled on, reaching a peak shortly after Lardner's death in 1933. However stated, the central keynote running through all the death notices was that "with the death of Ring Lardner, one of the really important figures in our contemporary literature passes."[19]

While acquiring recognition as a serious writer, Lardner never lost his earlier reputation as a humorist. He was in fact frequently hailed as one of the leading American humorists,[20] and that he deserved a dual reputation as both a serious and a humorous writer is of course fully supported by the works he wrote. At the

[145]

same time, in an age which rediscovered Melville's tragic vision, reassessed Mark Twain as a pessimist, and applauded the harsh realism of Dreiser and Lewis, critics more and more came to lay heavy stress on Lardner's satire, which of course merited stress. But perhaps primarily as the result of Lardner's reticence about himself and his aims and of his objective methods by which he avoided dealing with the subjective states of his characters, critics began interpreting his satiric attitude as one of cold hatred. Clifton Fadiman became a prime mover in promoting this viewpoint, though he by no means stood alone. In 1929, Fadiman contended that "Lardner is the deadliest because the coldest of American writers. Unlike Sinclair Lewis he is without a soft streak. He really hates his characters, hates them so much that he has ceased to be indignant at them. . . . His satire is absolutely negative; that is why it will never cause a revolution in American manners, as 'Main Street,' in a minor way, did." And he saw Lardner's "coldly contemptuous picture" as the product "merely of his own idiosyncratic temperament."[21]

From this start, Fadiman, a few years later, went on to propound a "triangle of hate" theory: Lardner's hatred of himself, of his characters, and his characters' hatred of each other. Fadiman reached the conclusion that Lardner was the possessor of a "perfectly clear simon-pure, deliberate misanthropy," the proof of which was that Lardner had populated his fictional world with "mental sadists, four-flushers, intolerable gossipers, meal-ticket females, interfering morons, brainless flirts, liars, brutes, spiteful snobs, vulgar climbers, dishonest jockeys, selfish children, dipsomaniacal chorus girls, senile chatterers, idiotically complacent husbands, mean arrivistes, drunks, snoopers, poseurs, and bridge players."[22]

In the meantime in 1932, and thus before the appearance of Fadiman's second article, Ludwig Lewisohn, who was among the first literary historians to give Lardner a definite rank in the tradition of American literature, had in his *Expression in America* taken a position similar to Fadiman's. Emphasizing, as Fadiman had, Lardner's supposedly "icy hatred and contempt," Lewisohn held that his "bitter and brutal stories belong not only to literature but to the history of civilization." Moreover to Lewisohn "the cream of Lardner's ferocious jesting" was that "he had been able to sell his merciless tales to the periodicals that cater to the very fools and rogues whom he castigates."[23]

This critical stereotype was further established by Maxwell Geismar, who published the first extended analysis of Lardner's work in his *Writers in Crisis* (1942). Looking more directly to Fadiman than to Lewisohn, Geismar contended that Lardner refuted the "national faiths" without offering solutions to our problems, and that thus he had "no purpose in his anger, . . . no positive to his hatred, and . . . no destination beyond destruction." As the result of this complete negativism, a "pattern of . . . hatred" ran through his fiction, wherein "in a sort of compulsive design Lardner creates indestructible characters whom he vainly attempts to destroy." And Geismar goes on: "Here is a ceaseless masochism which illuminates the painfully divided personality of an author continually tearing down what he is in the process of building up, who, in short, is unable to accept what he has made of himself."[24] Finally, though taking a less extreme view than Geismar or Fadiman, Henry Steele Commager promoted the "hatred" theory as recently as 1950 in *The American Mind,* saying that Lardner seared all his characters "with impartial hatred" and was "above all the historian of frustration."[25]

This critical viewpoint, particularly as represented in the extreme positions taken by Fadiman and Geismar, is manifestly absurd. It would invite the reader to view Lardner as a mental sadist, as a writer with no aim except that of pouring out a helpless and hopeless anger, and as a person with no ideal or principle of any sort. Viewed thus, his work would have to be dismissed as the product of a distorted vision and as lacking a basis in real life. It must, of course, be conceded that Lardner showed an intense dislike for some of the characters he created, of which the vicious Midge Kelly is the outstanding example, and that he was a satirist and therefore consistently engaged in censuring the wrong behavior, the defective values, and the coarseness and vulgarity of many others of his characters. But as a satirist concerned, as any satirist must be, with the deviations of life and human conduct from at least an imaginary if not an actual and commonly accepted ideal, Lardner had to operate from the basis of a set of values and principles.

The objectivity of his method which typically resulted in his presenting in a story only the negative side of the picture—that is, only the deviation from the ideal standard and not the standard itself, which is usually only implied—perhaps explains why Fadiman and Geismar found "no positive" to what they regarded as

Lardner's hatred. They simply overlooked or totally disregarded the obvious: that in every case Lardner's "negative" implied a "positive"—not an obscure, mysterious positive, but a commonly accepted, plainly apparent one which Lardner reasonably expected the reader to possess already or to comprehend from the story. This is no more than other writers, using the objective method and concerning themselves primarily with the external behavior of their characters, expect of a reader.

The two scholars who have done the most to clear up the Fadiman-Geismar distortion and to enable one to understand Lardner's real temperament, as well as the specific nature of the conflict he had with his society, are Howard W. Webb and Donald Elder. In an unpublished dissertation written in 1953, Webb supported the position that "Lardner's basic norm was his unswerving conviction that there must be respect for the dignity and worth and integrity of the individual,"[26] a conviction he never lost. One of the primary themes Elder stressed in his biography of Lardner (published in 1956) was that Lardner was not merely an idealist but one with a decided puritan cast of mind, whose relationships with his fellow man were governed by a strong personal code of honor. Lardner's close associates, Elder affirmed, regarded him as "an exceptionally magnanimous and loving man" who had no hatred for the human race "but only for meanness, falseness, and pretentiousness" (317). The "hate" theory, therefore, is untenable. Instead of being viewed as a misanthrope Lardner can rather be viewed as a writer motivated at least to some degree by the idealistic hope that human improvement begins with self-knowledge, with an awareness of one's defects and shortcomings.

II *Lardner's Literary Position*

If there has been critical dissent about Lardner's aims and attitudes, there has never been the least suggestion of dispute regarding what possibly deserves recognition as the single most distinguishing feature of his work: namely, that it belongs wholly to the native American literary tradition. All critics, early or late, are in agreement that he pictured only distinctly American character types—ones who talk, think, and act American—and that his method and style were also thoroughly in the native tradition. He was himself perhaps unaware of how completely he was immersed in this tradition, for he wrote about the phases of American life which came under his observation and of which he was himself a part. The very fact that he presented an unflattering image of America through his competitive, egotistical, selfish, and, in a few cases, even brutal characters may be taken as a further indication of his Americanism. For many of the writers now most closely identified with the native tradition have also been numbered among its sharpest critics: for example, Mark Twain, Sherwood Anderson, H. L. Mencken, and Sinclair Lewis. In *Democratic Vistas,* even the expansively optimistic Walt Whitman censured many of the identical defects of American life which Lardner satirized in his fiction. Few others have concerned themselves so consistently with what Whitman described as the "dry and flat Sahara" of American life as Lardner did, but the difference is in degree, not in intent.

The fact that Lardner's fiction is thus firmly anchored in the native American tradition, however, returns us to Mencken's speculation that it might become dated as the result of the passing from American life of the character types he depicted and of the vernacular idiom he used extensively. So far there is no indication that such a fate is overtaking Lardner's fiction, and it is highly doubtful that it ever will; for Lardner was no local colorist concerning himself with the characters and the language peculiar to a restricted locality or even to a region. While all his characters are particularized and specific, most of them are common American types who belong to the mainstream of American society rather than to some special current or eddy of it, and the language they speak is the common American language, neither dialect nor slang, but the living language of the rank and file American. As many commentators have noted, the special force of Lardner's fiction lies in the fact that he perceived and captured in it the character types newly emerging from the materialistic, business-dominated society of his era. While it would be interesting to speculate whether these types and the language they spoke have since become more or less dominant in American society, the significant fact is that fiction which authentically mirrors important and distinctive phases of the life of its author's day makes a claim for permanent interest, as is clearly the case with Mark Twain's. Thus, contrary to what Mencken thought, the strongly native cast of Lardner's fiction doubtless will do much to give it a lasting appeal.

Despite the close identification of Lardner's fiction with his own time and place, it nevertheless treats broad and universal themes. Those of nearly all his best stories, for example, center on various forms of egotism such as vanity, pride, self-obsession, and the thoughtless or malicious intrusion of one person into another's life. These themes have concerned other American writers, notably Hawthorne and Henry James. Of course, it would hardly be possible to conceive of a greater contrast than exists between Lardner's fictional world and that of Hawthorne or James. In Lardner's, there are no Ethan Brands tramping around the world in search of the unpardonable sin hidden in their own hearts, no Roderick Ellistons conversing with the serpents they carry in their bosoms, no John Marchers waiting for a great event to spring on them as a beast in the jungle springs on its prey, and no governesses on country estates terrorized by frightful apparitions. Instead, Lardner's world is a commonplace, nearby, real one, ungarnished by symbolism and exotic settings, and populated by blustering Jack Keefes, wise-cracking Gullibles, tongue-wagging females, and nasty-tempered bridge players. Furthermore, both Hawthorne and James were concerned with the interior workings of their characters' minds, but Lardner primarily limited himself to reporting the external behavior of his characters, making the characters reveal their subjective states and motives through their actions and speech. Neither his objective method nor the everyday commonplaceness of his characters should be allowed to obscure the fact that he treated in his fiction serious, fundamental themes which have a vital bearing on the human predicament. He treated them in his own method in terms of the world he knew and lived in and through the unheroic characters and events typical of that world. This fact enhances the gravity of his statement, for his world is the one in which Americans still live.

The question of what rank Ring Lardner has earned in the tradition of American literature has no categorical answer. Obviously, he is not to be bracketed with the greatest masters of American fiction, but just as obviously he deserves a more important position than literary historians have yet assigned to him. But as this chapter has sought to indicate, he has been accorded consistently favorable critical appreciation, and his reputation now appears to be solidly established and growing. As time passes and more of his uncollected fiction is made readily accessible in book form, there seems little doubt that he will be established among the most important American writers of the early twentieth century and among the foremost masters of the American short story.

Notes and References

Chapter One

1. Donald Elder, *Ring Lardner, A Biography* (Garden City, 1956), p. 12. Much of the factual information contained in this chaper is derived from this biography, though original sources have also been used, as will be indicated. Hereafter citations to the Elder biography will be made in the text.

2. Ring Lardner, "Me, Boy Scout," *Saturday Evening Post*, November 21, 1931, p. 5.

3. Ring Lardner, "What I Ought to of Learnt in High School," *American Magazine*, XCVI (November, 1923), 10. Other quotations in this paragraph are from the same source.

4. *Ibid.*, p. 82.

5. "Ring Lardner-Himself," *Saturday Evening Post*, April 28, 1917, p. 45.

6. *Ibid.*

7. Thomas L. Masson, "Ring Lardner," *Our American Humorists* (New York, 1922), p. 207.

8. Ring Lardner, "Meet Mr. Howley," *Saturday Evening Post*, November 14, 1931, p. 12.

9. Masson, *op. cit.*, p. 207.

10. *Ibid.*

11. See Elder, p. 34. See also Sherwood Anderson, "Meeting Ring Lardner," *No Swank* (Philadelphia, 1934), p. 1.

12. Lardner gives this account in "Meet Mr. Howley," *op. cit.*, p. 12.

13. "Ring Lardner-himself," *op. cit.*, p. 48.

14. "Stoll Gave Lardner First Writing Job," *Editor and Publisher*, LXVI (October 14, 1933), 30.

15. Ring Lardner, "Alias James Clarkson," *Saturday Evening Post*, April 16, 1932, p. 108.

16. *Ibid.*

17. See Elder, p. 78. See also Howard W. Webb, Jr., "The Lardner Idiom," *American Quarterly*, XII (Winter, 1960), 483.

18. See letters quoted by Elder, pp. 58, 76.

19. *Op. cit.*, pp. 485-89.

20. See T. S. Matthews, "Lardner, Shakespeare, and Chekhov," *New Republic*, LIX (May 22, 1929), 35-36.

21. "Ring Lardner: Highbrow in Hiding," *Reporter*, August 9, 1956, p. 52.

22. H. L. Mencken, "A Humorist Shows His Teeth," *The American Mercury*, VIII (June, 1926), 255.

23. "Ring," *New Republic*, October 11, 1933, p. 255.

24. Quoted in Elder, pp. 184-85.

25. Quoted by Howard W. Webb, Jr., in his unpublished dissertation, *Ring Lardner's Conflict and Reconciliation with American Society* (Iowa, 1953), p. 157.

26. Clifton Fadiman, "Ring Lardner and the Triangle of Hate," *Nation*, CXXXVI (March 22, 1933), 315.

27. "Ring Lardner Left $192,927 . . ." New York *Herald Tribune*, May 13, 1934.

28. See Fitzgerald, "Ring," *op. cit.;* Lardner's "Why Authors?" in his *What of it?*, and Elder, pp. 243-91.

29. Fitzgerald, *op. cit.*, p. 254.

30. "Three Stories a Year Are Enough for a Writer," *New York Times*, March 25, 1917 (Book review section), p. 14.

31. Quoted in Elder, p. 51.

32. Fadiman, *op. cit.*, p. 315.

33. Edmund Wilson, "Ring Lardner's American Characters," *A Literary Chronicle: 1920-1950* (an Anchor paperback) (New York, 1956), p. 37.

34. Harry Salpeter, "The Boswell of New York," *The Bookman,* LXXXI (July, 1930), 384.

35. Webb, Dissertation, *op. cit.*, pp. 215-16.

36. "Ring," *op. cit.*, p. 254.

37. Ring Lardner, "Lyricists Strike Pay Dirt," *New Yorker*, November 19, 1932, p. 53.

38. "Ring," *op. cit.*, p. 255.

39. "Ring Lardner," *No Swank*, p. 1.

40. "Ring," *op. cit.*, p. 255.

41. "Four American Impressions," *Notebook* (New York, 1926), p. 51.

42. "American Fiction," *The Moment and other Essays* (London, 1952), p. 101.

Chapter Two

1. *March 6th: The Home Coming of Charles A. Comiskey, John J. McGraw, and James J. Callahan* (Chicago, 1914).

2. *Portable Ring Lardner* (New York, 1946), p. 4.

3. *You Know Me Al,* pp. 9-10. All references are to the 1925 Scribner edition.

4. See, for example, Stuart Sherman, "Ring Lardner: Hard-boiled Americans," *The Main Stream* (New York, 1927), pp. 171-72.

5. *Op. cit.,* p. 102.

6. "Americana," *New Republic,* October 11, 1946, p. 488.

7. *Portable Ring Lardner,* p. 5.

8. *Treat 'Em Rough* (Indianapolis, 1918), pp. 154, 157.

9. *The Real Dope* (Indianapolis, 1919), p. 72.

10. "The Busher Re-enlists," *Saturday Evening Post,* April 19, 1919, p. 10.

11. *Portable Ring Lardner,* p. 5.

12. "Alias James Clarkson," *op. cit.,* p. 108.

13. Carl Van Doren, "Beyond Grammar: Ring W. Lardner: Philologist among the Low-Brows," *Century,* CVI (July, 1923), 472.

14. See Elder, p. 123.

15. Doren, *op. cit.,* p. 475.

16. "What Is American about America?" *Harper's* magazine, (July, 1956), p. 28.

Chapter Three

1. *Op. cit.,* p. 317.

2. *Portable Lardner,* p. 12.

3. "The Swift Six," *Redbook,* XXVII (July, 1916), 549-50.

4. "Fore!," *Redbook,* XXIX (May, 1917), 38.

5. *"The Swift Six,"* p. 558.

6. "What Is the 'American Language'?," *Bookman,* LIII (March, 1921), 31.

7. *Ibid.*

8. *Portable Lardner,* p. 13.

9. "Ring Lardner's Bell Lettres," *Bookman,* CXII (September, 1925), 46.

10. "Tables for Two," *New Yorker,* October 18, 1930, p. 23.

Chapter Four

1. *Editor to Author: The Letters of Maxwell E. Perkins,* ed. by John Hall Wheelock (New York, 1950), p. 37.

2. All quotations refer to the 1924 Scribner's edition.

3. Thomas L. Masson, "Simple, Isn't It?," *Bookman,* XLVIIII (February, 1919), 709.

4. "Ring," p. 255.

5. "Ring Lardner's American's Characters," p. 39.

6. *The Portable Lardner,* p. 7.

7. See Elder, pp. 209-10.

8. "Ring Lardner and the Triangle of Hate," p. 316.

9. Quoted in Elder, pp. 210-11.

10. "The Meaning of Ring Lardner's Fiction: A Re-evaluation," *American Literature,* XXXI (January, 1960), 440-43, *passim.*

11. See Elder, p. 216.

12. *Op. cit.,* p. 36.

13. "Ring Lardner," *The New Republic,* September 3, 1924, p. 25.

Chapter Five

1. "Ring Lardner and the Triangle of Hate," p. 317.

2. "Ring Lardner's 'Ex Parte,'" *Reading Modern Short Stories* (Chicago, 1955), p. 50.

Chapter Six

1. Lardner is known to have published at least one other story, and there may be a few others among his unidentified writings. Further, under a very broad definition of the short story, two of his humorous narratives, "Second Act Curtain" and "In Conference," might be classified as short stories.

2. "Sick 'Em" (see list of uncollected stories in bibliography).

3. "The Crook"

4. "The Hold Out"

5. "The Yellow Kid"

6. "Battle of the Century," *Saturday Evening Post,* October 29, 1921, p. 86.

7. *Ibid.*

8. *Redbook,* February, 1918, p. 78.

9. *Ibid.,* p. 106.

10. Howard Webb, Jr. developed this point at some length. See *Ring Lardner's Conflict and Reconciliation with American Society,* pp. 222-23.

11. *Hearst's International Cosmopolitan,* September, 1927, p. 202.

12. *Ibid.,* p. 201.

13. *Esquire,* February, 1934, p. 18.

14. *Hearst's International Cosmopolitan,* December, 1929, p. 79.

15. *Delineator,* January, 1934, p. 32.

16. *Hearst's International Cosmopolitan,* May, 1931, p. 81.

Chapter Seven

1. I am disregarding *Zanzibar,* for which Lardner wrote the music and some of the lyrics, as well as the 1914 souvenir booklet commemorating the homecoming of the Giants and White Sox from their world tour.

2. See Elder, p. 98.

3. "The Fate of the Funny Men," *Bookman,* June, 1923, p. 457.

4. Quoted here from *First and Last,* pp. 27-28.

5. Gilbert Seldes, Preface, p. v.

6. See Howard Webb, *Ring Lardner's Conflict and Reconciliation with American Society,* p. 157; and Elder, pp. 94-112.

7. "The Story of a Wonder Man" (review), *The Dial,* September, 1927, p. 266.

Chapter Eight

1. Mencken republished this essay in his *Prejudices: Fifth Series* (New York, 1926); the quotations are from pp. 49-50 of this work.

2. Carl Van Doren and Stuart Sherman (see bibliography).

3. "Ring Lardner Dies After Long Illness," *Editor and Publisher,* September 30, 1933, p. 57.

4. "Ring Lardner—Serious Artist," *Bookman,* February, 1922, p. 586.

5. "Four American Impressions," *Notebook,* p. 50. The essay was first published in the *New Republic,* October 11, 1922.

6. *The American Language,* (2nd ed., New York, 1921), p. 276.

7. "Beyond Grammar: Ring W. Lardner: Philologist among the Low-Brows," *op. cit.,* p. 474.

8. *Op. cit.,* p. 39.

9. "Ring Lardner," *New Republic,* September 3, 1924, p. 25.

10. "Ring Lardner as Satirist," *Nation,* May 26, 1926, p. 584.

11. "A Humorist Shows His Teeth," *American Mercury,* June, 1926, pp. 254-55.

12. "Ring Lardner: Hardboiled Americans," *op. cit.,* p. 170.

13. "How to Write Short Stories" (review), *Outlook,* September 17, 1924, p. 100.

14. Littell, *op. cit.,* p. 25.

15. Allan Nevins, "The American Moron," *Saturday Review of Literature,* June 8, 1929, p. 1090.

16. *Op. cit.,* pp. 37-40, *passim.*

17. "Ring," pp. 254-55.

18. Harry Salpeter, "The Boswell of New York," *The Bookman,* July, 1930, p. 384.

19. "Ring Lardner," *Commonweal,* October 6, 1933, p. 518.

20. For an interesting discussion of Lardner's dual reputation, see Gilbert Seldes, "The Singular—Although Dual—Eminence of Ring Lardner," *American Criticism,* ed. by William A. Drake (New York, 1926) pp. 222-30.

21. "Pitiless Satire," *The Nation,* May 1, 1929, p. 537.

22. "Ring Lardner and the Triangle of Hate," pp. 315, 317.

23. (New York, 1932), pp. 514-15.

24. (Boston, 1942), pp. 12-13; 30.

25. (New Haven, 1950), p. 264.

26. *Ring Lardner's Conflict and Reconciliation with American Society,* pp. 1, 3.

Selected Bibliography

Selected Bibliography

PRIMARY SOURCES

The following listing of the first editions of the more important books and of the uncollected short stories is based on the extensive (but not yet definitive) bibliography compiled by Howard Webb, Jr. The greater portion of this bibliography appeared in Donald Elder's *Ring Lardner*, pp. 379-86.

Books (First Editions)

March 6th: The Home Coming of Charles A. Comiskey, John J. McGraw, and James J. Callahan. (With Edward C. Heeman.) Chicago: The Blakely Printing Co., 1914.

Bib Ballads. Chicago: P. F. Volland and Company, 1915.

You Know Me Al. New York: George H. Doran Company, 1916.

Gullible's Travels, Etc. Indianapolis: The Bobbs-Merrill Company, 1917.

My Four Weeks in France. Indianapolis: The Bobbs-Merrill Company, 1918.

Treat 'Em Rough. Indianapolis: The Bobbs-Merrill Company, 1918.

Own Your Own Home. Indianapolis: The Bobbs-Merrill Company, 1919.

The Real Dope. Indianapolis: The Bobbs-Merrill Company, 1919.

Regular Fellows I Have Met. Chicago: Wilmont, 1919.

The Young Immigrunts. Indianapolis: The Bobbs-Merrill Company, 1920.

Symptoms of Being 35. Indianapolis: The Bobbs-Merrill Company, 1921.

The Big Town. Indianapolis: The Bobbs-Merrill Company, 1921.

Say It with Oil. New York: George H. Doran Company, 1923.

How to Write Short Stories [With Samples]. New York: Charles Scribner's Sons, 1924.

What of It? New York: Charles Scribner's Sons, 1925.

The Love Nest and Other Stories. New York: Charles Scribner's Sons, 1926.

The Story of a Wonder Man. New York: Charles Scribner's Sons, 1927.

Round Up. New York: Charles Scribner's Sons, 1929.

June Moon. (With George S. Kaufman.) New York: Charles Scribner's
 Sons, 1930.

Lose with a Smile. New York: Charles Scribner's Sons, 1933.

First and Last. Edited by Gilbert Seldes. New York: Charles Scribner's
 Sons, 1934.

Uncollected Short Stories

A. *Sequence Groups*

"The Busher Abroad," *Saturday Evening Post,* CLXXXVII (March
 20, 1915), 19-21, 57-58; CLXXXVII (April 10, 1915), 20-22,
 73-74; CLXXXVII (May 8, 1915), 20-22, 65-67; CLXXXVII
 (May 15, 1915), 25-27, 77-78; "The Busher's Welcome Home,"
 Saturday Evening Post, CLXXXVII (June 5, 1915), 18-20, 52-54.

"War Bribes," *Redbook,* XXVI (April, 1916), 1111-21.

"The Swift Six," *Redbook,* XXVII (July, 1916), 549-60.

"Fore!," *Redbook,* XXIX (May, 1917), 35-46.

"Call for Mr. Keefe," *Saturday Evening Post,* CXC (March 9, 1918),
 3-4, 78, 80, 82. (Belongs with the *Treat 'Em Rough* group).

"The Busher Re-enlists," *Saturday Evening Post,* CXCI (April 19,
 1919), 3-4, 147, 151, 155.

"The Battle of Texas," *Saturday Evening Post,* CXCI (May 24, 1919),
 12-13, 94, 98.

"Along Came Ruth," *Saturday Evening Post,* CXCII (July 26, 1919),
 12-13, 120, 123.

"The Courtship of T. Dorgan," *Saturday Evening Post,* CXCII
 (September 6, 1919), 8-9, 173-74, 177.

"The Busher Pulls a Mays," *Saturday Evening Post,* CXCII (October
 13, 1919), 16-17, 182, 185-86.

B. *Separate Short Stories*

"Sick 'Em," *Saturday Evening Post,* CLXXXVII (July 25, 1914), 16-18,
 33-35.

"Back to Baltimore," *Redbook,* XXIV (November, 1914), 29-14.

"Tour No. 2," (In Two Parts), *Saturday Evening Post,* CLXXXVII
 (February 13, 1915), 16-18, 41-42; CLXXXVII (February 20,
 1915), 21-23, 41-42.

"The Poor Simp," *Saturday Evening Post,* CLXXXVIII (September
 11, 1915), 16-18, 61-62.

"Where Do You Get That Noise?," *Saturday Evening Post,* CLXXXVIII
 (October 23, 1915), 10-12, 40-41.

"Oh, You Bonehead," *Saturday Evening Post,* CLXXXVIII (October
 30, 1915), 16-17, 45.

"Good for the Soul," *Saturday Evening Post, CLXXXVIII* (March
 25, 1916), 20-23, 78, 81-82.

"The Crook," *Saturday Evening Post*, CLXXXVIII (June 24, 1916), 18-20, 52.

"A One-Man Team," *Redbook*, XXVIII (November, 1916), 93-103.

"Tour-Y-10," *Metropolitan*, XLV (February, 1917), 12-14, 34, 39-40; 42-43.

"The Hold-Out," *Saturday Evening Post*, CLXXXIX (March 24, 1917), 8-10, 49-50.

"A Friendly Game," *Saturday Evening Post*, CLXXXIX (May 5, 1917), 10-12, 53, 55.

"Ball-A-Hole," *Saturday Evening Post*, CLXXXIX (May 12, 1917), 16-18, 75, 78.

"The Yellow Kid," *Saturday Evening Post*, CLXXXIX (June 23, 1917), 8-10, 69.

"The Last Night," *Redbook*, XXX (November, 1917), 95-100.

"The Clubby Roadster," *Redbook*, XXX (February, 1918), 61-65.

"A Chip of the Old Block," *Redbook*, XXX (September, 1918), 76-79, 106, 108.

"The Battle of the Century," *Saturday Evening Post* (October 29, 1921), 12, 84, 86.

"The Jade Necklace," *Hearst's International Cosmopolitan*, LXXXI (November, 1926), 28-3'.

"The Spinning Wheel," *Hearst's International Cosmopolitan*, LXXXIII (July, 1927), 106-8, 111.

"The Venomous Viper of the Volga," *Hearst's International Cosmopolitan*, LXXXIII (September, 1927), 52-53, 198-202.

"Wedding Day," *Hearst's International Cosmopolitan*, LXXXV (July, 1928), 66-69.

"Absent-Minded Beggar," *Hearst's International Cosmopolitan*, LXXXVI (March, 1929), 70-71, 186, 188-92.

"High-Rollers," *Hearst's International Cosmopolitan*, LXXXVI (June, 1929), 76-77, 108, 110.

"Stop Me—If You've Heard This One," *Hearst's International Cosmopolitan*, LXXXVII (July, 1929), 98-99, 122, 124.

"Pity Is Akin," *Hearst's International Cosmopolitan*, LXXXVII (September, 1929), 74-75, 161-62.

"That Old Sweetheart of Mine," *Hearst's International Cosmopolitan*, LXXXVII (November, 1929), 34-35, 166, 168-69.

"Great Blessings," *Hearst's International Cosmopolitan*, LXXXVII (December, 1929), 79-81, 132.

"Mamma," *Good Housekeeping*, XC (June, 1930), 52-54, 252.

"Words and Music," *Good Housekeeping*, XCI (August, 1930), 30-33, 173-74.

"Cured!," *Redbook*, LVI (March, 1931), 41-45, 124.

"Insomnia," *Hearst's International Cosmopolitan*, XC (May, 1931), 81-83.

"Take A Walk," *American*, CXVI (October, 1933), 66-69, 106, 109.
"Bob's Birthday," *Redbook*, LXII (November, 1933), 36-37, 75.
"Poodle," *Delineator*, CXXIV (January, 1934), 8-9, 30, 32.
"Greek Tragedy," *Esquire*, I (February, 1934), 18-19, 85, 147.
"Widow," *Redbook*, LXV (October, 1935), 28-31, 65.
"Freedom of the Press," *Pictorial Review*, XXXVII (November, 1935), 14-15, 43, 44.
"How Are You?," *Redbook*, LXVI (December, 1935), 22-25, 83.

SECONDARY SOURCES

Only significant or representative discussions are listed. The dissertations by James R. Frakes and Howard W. Webb, Jr. (see below) contain extensive bibliographies.

Book

ELDER, DONALD. *Ring Lardner, A Biography* (Garden City: Doubleday and Co., 1956). Gives an exhaustive account of Lardner's life, evaluates his work, and includes a chronologically arranged bibliography of his publications.

Unpublished Studies

CLARK ISAAC E. *An Analysis of Ring Lardner's American Language, or Who Learnt You Grammer Bud?* (Master's thesis, University of Texas, 1944). Gives a detailed analysis of Lardner's rendering of the American vulgate.

FRAKES, JAMES RICHARD. *Ring Lardner: A Critical Survey* (Doctoral dissertation, University of Pennsylvania, 1953). Examines Lardner's career and work chronologically; is one of the first two extended evaluations of Lardner's achievement.

WEBB, HOWARD WILLIAM, JR. *Ring Lardner's Conflict and Reconciliation with American Society* (Doctoral dissertation, Iowa, 1953). Interprets Lardner's work in the light of the conflict it reflects between his values and beliefs and those of his society, the relation shifting from period to period.

Essays

ANDERSON, SHERWOOD. "Four American Impressions: Gertrude Stein, Paul Rosenfeld, Ring Lardner, Sinclair Lewis," *The New Republic*, XXXII (October 11, 1922), 171-73. Reprinted in *Sherwood Anderson's Notebook* (New York, 1926, pp. 47-55). Stresses Lardner's sympathetic understanding of life, his shyness, and his sensitivity.

————. "Meeting Ring Lardner," *The New Yorker,* IX (November 25, 1933), 36, 38. Reprinted in *No Swank* (Philadelphia, pp. 1-7). Makes a vivid commentary on Lardner's temperament and personality.

BENCHLEY, ROBERT C. "The Fate of the Funny Men," *Bookman,* LVII (June, 1923), 455-57. Thinks *Say It with Oil* was a magazine editor's idea of humor rather than Lardner's.

BERRYMAN, JOHN. "The Case of Ring Lardner," *Commentary,* XXII (November, 1956), 416-23. Advances the questionable viewpoint that Lardner's best work is the "accident of talent," that it showed no invention, imagination, or sense of structure, and only a limited sense of style.

BOYD, THOMAS. "Lardner Tells Some New Ones," *Bookman,* LIX (July, 1924), 601-2. Sees Lardner's characters as sharp entities, taken from the great mass "in which he, himself, is rooted."

BIBESCO, E. "Lament for Lardner," *Living Age,* CCCXXXXV (December, 1933), 366-68. Holds that Lardner made a "devastating" indictment of American civilization and that he was a greater artist than Sinclair Lewis.

CHAMBERLAIN, JOHN. "Ring Lardner Listens in on the Life About Him," New York *Times* "Book Review" (April 7, 1929), p. 2. Calls Lardner "our best short story writer."

DOUGLAS, DONALD. "Ring Lardner As Satirist," *The Nation,* CXXII (May 26, 1926), 584-85. Sees *Love Nest* as a reflection of Lardner's "increasing irony and bitterness"; fairly representative of the laudatory reviews of *Love Nest* and of the viewpoint many critics took of Lardner during the mid-1920's.

FADIMAN, CLIFTON. "Pitiless Satire," *Nation,* CXXVIII (May 1, 1929), 536-37. A first statement of the viewpoint more fully developed in "The Triangle of Hate" (see below).

————. "Ring Lardner and the Triangle of Hate" *Nation,* CXXXVI (March 22, 1933), 315-17. An essay which influenced other critics, takes extreme and unsupportable view that Lardner was a misanthrope, hating his characters, himself, and depicting his characters as hating each other.

FARRELL, JAMES T. "Ring Lardner's Success Mad World," New York *Times* "Book Review" (June, 1944), pp. 3, 18. Reprinted as "Ring Lardner's *Round Up,*" *The League of Frightened Philistines and Other Papers.* New York: The Vanguard Press, 1945. An interesting discussion of *Round Up;* it holds that the intense competitiveness of Lardner's characters "reveals the working out of the mechanisms" of the competitive American system.

FITZGERALD, F. SCOTT. "Ring," *The New Republic,* LXXVI (October 11, 1933), 254-55. Interesting but highly subjective interpretation of Lardner's attitudes and apparent lack of interest in his work.

GEISMAR, MAXWELL. "Ring Lardner: Like Something was Going to Happen," *Writers in Crisis, The American Novel Between Two Wars.* Boston: Houghton, Mifflin Co., 1942. One of the first extended discussions of Lardner's fiction, it gives a distorted interpretation by holding that Lardner despised his characters and himself, that "a ceaseless masochism" pervades his work.

LEWISOHN, LUDWIG. *Expression in America.* New York: Harper and Brothers, 1932. Describes Lardner as a "neo-naturalist"; sees his "bitter and brutal stories" as belonging "not only to literature but to the history of civilization."

LITTELL, ROBERT. "Ring Lardner," *The New Republic,* XL (September 3, 1924), 25-26. Praises Lardner's handling of the American idiom and his ability "to write our diaries for us."

MASSON, THOMAS L. "Ring Lardner," *Our American Humorists.* New York: Moffat, Yard and Co., 1922). Views Lardner as "an American humorist of no mean proportions."

MATTHEWS, T. S. "Lardner, Shakespeare, and Chekhov," *New Republic,* LIX (May 22, 1929), 35-36. Compares Lardner with Shakespeare and Chekhov on the basis that all three had both a serious and a popular audience.

MENCKEN, HENRY L. *The American Language: An Inquiry into the Development of English in the United States.* 2nd ed., revised and enlarged. New York: Knopf 1921. Contains a laudatory discussion of Lardner's rendering of common American speech (pp. 274-77); includes a sample of his "baseball-American" (pp. 404-5).

————. "Lardner," *Prejudices, Fifth Series.* New York: Knopf, 1926. Contends that the professors will take up Lardner only after the changing pattern of American civilization has made his idiom and characters obsolete.

————. "A Humorist Shows His Teeth," *The American Mercury,* VIII (June, 1926), 354-55. Finds *The Love Nest and Other Stories* filled with satire of "the most acid and appalling sort"; commends Lardner for "trying to get the low-down Americano between covers."

NEVINS, ALLAN. "The American Moron," *Saturday Review of Literature,* V (June 8, 1929), 1089-90. Compares Lardner's rise from sports writing and humor to serious literature with O. Henry's from-prison-to fame story, and with Mark Twain's rise from the ranks of funny men to serious literature.

OVERTON, GRANT. "Ring W. Lardner's Belle Lettres," *Bookman,* LXII (September, 1925), 44-49. A somewhat facetious essay on the collected edition of Lardner's work; Overton interviewed Lardner and the essay does give some relevant information.

SALPETER, HARRY. "The Boswell of New York," *The Bookman,* LXXXI

(July, 1930), 384. Reports that Lardner denied that he was a satirist, that he just listened.

SCHWARTZ, DELMORE. "Ring Lardner: Highbrow in Hiding," *Reporter*, XV (August 9, 1956), pp. 52-54. Thinks that it "is clear that there was a kind of puritanism at the heart of [Lardner's] work—an innocent purity of heart and mind that was . . . appalled by the unfulfilled promises of life."

SELDES, GILBERT. "The Singular—Although Dual—Eminence of Ring Lardner," *American Criticism*. William A. Drake, ed. New York: Harcourt, Brace, 1926. Discusses the singularity of Lardner's dual standing as a "funny man" admired by a popular audience and as a satirist admired by the *"cognoscenti."*

————. "Editor's Introduction," *The Portable Ring Lardner*. New York: The Viking Press, 1946. An excellent general commentary on Lardner.

————. "Mr. Dooley, Meet Mr. Lardner," *The Seven Lively Arts*. New York: Harper and Brothers, 1957. A reprint of an essay which first appeared in this volume in 1924, with added comments, revising the earlier viewpoint and contending that "the really memorable things" of Lardner's are "the stories and fantasies."

SHERMAN, STUART. "Ring Lardner: Hardboiled Americans," *The Main Stream*. New York: Charles Scribner's Sons, 1927. Describes Lardner as a "hard-boiled realist" but errs in regarding the facetious prefaces to *How to Write Short Stories* and *The Love Nest* as an indication that Lardner did not take his "hard-boiled Americans . . . seriously."

STUART, HENRY LONGAN. "Mr. Lardner Burlesques America," New York *Times* "Book Review" (April 19, 1925), pp. 1, 25. Makes interesting comments on Lardner's nonsense plays.

————. "Three Stories A Year Are Enough For A Writer," New York *Times* Magazine (March 25, 1917), p. 14. Reports an interview with Lardner; indicates that he was tired of writing first-person dialect stories as early as 1917; quotes him as saying that he would like to be writing fiction "of an entirely different sort from that which I write now."

THURSTON, JARVIS A. "Ring Lardner's 'Ex Parte,'" *Reading Modern Short Stories*. Chicago: Scott, Foresman, 1955. A thorough and sound analysis of "Ex Parte."

VAN DOREN, CARL. "Beyond Grammar: Ring W. Lardner: Philologist among the Low-brows," *Century*, CVI (July, 1923), 471-75. Praises the vernacular style for its effectiveness in expressing the characters but considers Lardner as "essentially a comic philologist."

WEAVER, JOHN V. "Ring Lardner—Serious Artist," *The Bookman*, LIV

(February, 1922), 586-87. Shows that Lardner was already gaining a serious reputation in the early 1920's.

WEBB, HOWARD W., JR. "The Meaning of Ring Lardner's Fiction: A Re-Evaluation," *American Literature*, XXXI (January, 1960), 434-45. Develops the thesis that "the dominant theme" in Lardner's fiction was not "the pettiness and meanness of modern life" but "the problem of communication," the term "communication" being used in its broadest sense.

––––––. "Ring Lardner's Idle Common Man," *BCMVASA*, I (Spring, 1958), 6-13. Discusses the satire of white-collar workers found in Lardner's writings from 1913 to 1919.

WHEELOCK, JOHN HALL (ed.). *Editor to Author: The Letters of Maxwell Perkins*, New York: Charles Scribner's Sons, 1950. Reprints two interesting letters Perkins wrote Lardner in connection with *How to Write Short Stories*.

WILSON, EDMUND. "Mr. Lardner's American Characters," *Dial*, LXXVII (July, 1924), pp. 69-72. Reprinted in Edmund Wilson, *A Literary Chronicle: 1920-1950* (an Anchor book) (Garden City, 1956), pp. 37-40. Is a judicious appraisal of Lardner's work as reflected by the stories in *How to Write Short Stories*.

WOOLF, VIRGINIA. "American Fiction," *The Moment and Other Essays*. London: Hogarth Press, 1952. Contends that games provide "a centre" for Lardner's fiction.

Index

Index